Mission Me 2.0

Mission Me 2.0
The Science and Soul of Coming Back to You

Crystal Robinson

Published by Game Changer Publishing

Paperback ISBN: 978-1-968250-03-4
Hardcover ISBN: 978-1-968250-04-1
Digital ISBN: 978-1-968250-05-8

GC GAME CHANGER
PUBLISHING

www.GameChangerPublishing.com

For Brian,
who held the light steady when mine dimmed.
For every client, seeker, and soul I've had the honor of guiding.
This book is for the moments when you chose yourself,
even when it was the hardest thing to do.

Read This First

Thank you so much for picking up this book.
Before you dive in, I have something special for you.

I've created a few free gifts to support and inspire you as
you walk your own path of healing and transformation.

Scan the QR code to access your free gifts,
just my way of saying thank you and welcome.

You're not alone in this. Let's begin.

Mission Me 2.0

The Science and Soul of Coming Back to You

Crystal Robinson

Praise for *Mission Me 2.0*

"Mission Me 2.0 is a breathtakingly honest, deeply healing guide for anyone ready to stop performing and start truly living. Crystal's story is both vulnerable and empowering—a reminder that real transformation begins the moment we choose ourselves. She beautifully blends science and spirituality to illuminate a path back to authenticity, presence, and purpose. This book isn't just something you read—it's something you feel. A must-have for anyone on the journey of coming home to themselves."
—**Kristyn & Luisa**, *Flying Upstream* **Podcast**

"If you're on a journey of growth, personal development, and truly falling in love with who you are—inside and out—I wholeheartedly recommend Crystal Robinson's book. Crystal carries such a beautiful, grounding energy. Having her in my world, sharing conversations, and hearing her insights has been such a gift.

Her book is a powerful reflection of her own deeply personal journey, woven with wisdom, love, and transformational stories. She's poured so much heart and energy into these pages, and you can feel it. I've had the honor of featuring Crystal on my podcast, and each time we've connected, her presence brings clarity, inspiration, and truth.

This book is a beautiful place to start if you're ready to step into more of who you are. I know it will meet you exactly where you are and open you to meaningful breakthroughs."
—**Jo Warwick, Author, Healer, and Creator of the Rich, Sexy & Free Method**
Expert in Quantum Healing, Psychology, and Embodiment

"Mission Me 2.0 is more than a book, it's a lifeline for anyone who's lost themselves in the noise of obligation, burnout, or trauma. Crystal Robinson writes with a clarity, warmth, and compassion that makes you feel seen, not just as a reader, but as a whole person. Her integration of personal story, spiritual grounding, and evidence-based healing practices creates a deeply resonant guide for returning to your truest self. This is a powerful and necessary work for our times."
—**Tim Colligan, Founder, President, and CEO, StarSpring Consulting**

"Discovering Mission Me 2.0 and my why has been nothing short of transformative for me. At this pivotal stage in my life, this book and Crystal's sessions didn't just resonate—it gave language and clarity to feelings and questions I had long carried without form. She is helping me rediscover my purpose and reconnect with the deeper 'why' that fuels my evolution.

What makes this book truly impactful is the deeply thoughtful and integrative approach of its author, whose guidance has been instrumental in my journey. Her holistic understanding of the human experience—mind, body, and soul—shines through every page. She doesn't just offer insight; she offers a pathway to healing. Her work honors the complexity of what it means to be human, while gently urging the reader toward self-awareness, growth, and authenticity.

I am endlessly grateful for this work and the wisdom behind it. Mission Me 2.0 is more than a book—it's a compass for anyone seeking to align with their truth and evolve with intention."
—CT Thomas, *Co-Author of the Inspired Life Series*
(The Book on Joy, Transformation, Gratitude, Abundance, and Love)

"Mission Me 2.0 is a thoughtful and deeply personal guide to healing. Crystal shares her story with honesty and care, making space for both science and soul. Her words gently invite you back to yourself—without pressure, without perfection. This book is a reassuring companion for anyone navigating the messy, human path of becoming."
—**Meghann Dawson**, *Speaker, Coach, and Host of Becoming Is Messy*

"After reading Crystal's book Mission Me 2.0, I found her story so relatable. My 'aha' moment was realizing I had walked that very same path in my own journey. By doing the work and getting the guidance with Crystal, I was able to come out on the other side.

We all have 'stuff,' but I realized it was up to me to get that clarity and finally give myself the permission to move on ... to move forward and to feel better. Crystal gave me the tools I needed and continue to use. This has been truly amazing for me.

I finally live with BIG joy again."
—**Denise Hajjar**, *Fashion Designer*

"This is one of the most powerful and heartfelt books I have ever read. Crystal is a warrior who turned darkness into light—and shows you how to do the same. If you've had anything in your life that was not good for you and you've been seeking healing, begin with this book."
—**LS Kirkpatrick, *Award-Winning International Bestselling Author and Speaker***

"'Self-help' is a catchphrase that, by definition, suggests people have to do the work alone to get better and be better, by oneself. In her book, Crystal combines her personal experiences with effective strategies to support and guide you on your journey of self-discovery, healing, and personal growth—reminding you that you are not alone in your quest to become your true self."
—**Susan Francini, *Coaching Client and Early Reader***

"From Mission Me 2.0: 'Other times, the return feels like grief, like realizing how far you've drifted from the version of yourself you used to know. The one who used to dream, or laugh without needing to be productive, or sit still without guilt. It can be painful to notice the gap. But that noticing is powerful. Because it means you're already coming home. Coming back to yourself isn't a task to complete. It's a rhythm to remember.'

This passage really hit me. The image of 'coming home' to myself, not as a task but as a rhythm, stirred something deep within me. It made me pause and grieve the parts of myself I have intentionally left behind in the busyness of life. But more than anything, it offered me hope. Crystal's gentle reminder that noticing the distance is not failure but the first step of return— it's what I needed.

Crystal, thank you from the bottom of my heart for walking beside me through some of my toughest seasons. Your coaching has been more than support—it has been a lifeline. You helped me uncover clarity when I felt lost and reminded me of my strength when I couldn't see it myself. Most of all, you've helped me reconnect with my purpose, and for that, I will be forever grateful. Your impact on my life is something I'll carry with me always. And now, through this book, even more people will be touched by your wisdom, your light, and your gift."
—**Joanne Gagnon, RN, IBCLC, NTMNC, *Founder & CEO, Made of Gold Lactation***

"I had the pleasure of reading Crystal Robinson's book. It is chock full of information that will help anyone who is having physical, mental, or spiritual issues. In the book, there are many ideas on different modalities that will help the person struggling with these all-too-common problems. The book is well written and easy to read. It makes you rethink the problems that you are encountering and gives the reader advice that is practical to implement. She gives the reader an in-depth look at her own life and how the modalities she recommends have helped her become the person she is today. I highly recommend this book for anyone struggling with anxiety or depression."

—**Gary Sprouse, MD,** *The Less Stress Doc*

"Mission Me 2.0 is inspiring! Finally, a true guide on how to rediscover your authentic self. Crystal has a gentle way to help you dig deep to discover what really is important and clear away the 'stuff' that no longer serves you. You can feel Crystal's passion for healing on every page, as though she is walking right alongside you."

—**Teresa Lind, RN, NBC-HWC**

"Crystal is a wonderful writer. The flow of Mission Me 2.0 feels like walking beside her through a deeply personal and powerful journey—one challenge after another, with resilience and perseverance shining through every step. Her words aren't just coaching concepts or motivational phrases. They carry real emotion, lived experience, and heart.

This book beautifully captures what it means to shift from surviving to thriving. In a world driven by speed and instant gratification, Crystal invites us to pause, reflect, and ask the deeper questions. Her story challenges us to stop jumping from one thing to the next and instead learn how to live with intention and alignment

Mission Me 2.0 is for anyone who has never had an easy path but is ready to step into something more meaningful. It's inspiring, practical, and deeply human."

—**Chris Mamone**, *Acceptance Coach and Founder of The Empowered Grief Journey Podcast*

"Mission Me 2.0 is a transformative resource filled with actionable steps and practical exercises for ongoing self-development. Crystal's authentic personal stories drew me in immediately, and the framework provided will serve as a lasting tool for challenging my inner voice. Highly recommended for anyone committed to personal growth."

— **Jordan Callaghan**, *Entrepreneur and Online Fitness & Nutrition Coach*

"I've had the honor of being aligned with Crystal in business. With so much information out there, I definitely would dial in on what she is doing and accomplishing. As she moves her work worldwide, definitely engage in her book and other strategies."
—**Jim Lutes,** *Author and Publisher of The Change Book Series,* **President, Lutes International**

Foreword

It is my profound honor to introduce you to *Mission Me 2.0*, a book that feels, from its very first pages, like a sanctuary for the weary heart and the overburdened body.

I first met Crystal as a fellow traveler on the chronic-illness road. Like her, I was diagnosed with lupus. Many years ago, she discovered the community I'd built, reached out, and over time we forged a friendship rooted in mutual support, understanding, and transparency. I know intimately what it feels like when your body and nervous system cry out for safety. Crystal's gift is that she doesn't merely offer information—she creates an atmosphere of safety that readers can feel coursing through their nervous systems from her first few sentences.

One of the traits I love about Crystal is that she is unflinchingly authentic. In these pages, she lays bare her childhood wounds, the family expectations, and the misogyny she encountered in a male-dominated field—all of which conspired to fracture her physical and mental health. Yet she doesn't linger in pain; she guides us through it. She shows us how to hold our own trauma lightly, to recognize it as a voice asking for acknowledgment rather than a burden to be ashamed of.

What follows in *Mission Me 2.0* is neither a clinical textbook nor a spiritual lecture. Crystal weaves modern neuroscience and research with practices as ancient as the human spirit itself: somatic release, meditation, dance, energy work, boundary-setting, and the nourishment of body and soul. She maps a path from "doing" to "being," from survival to thriving, with compassion and rigor in equal measure.

There are so many aspects of *Mission Me 2.0* that make it extraordinary, including:

1. A Safe Harbor to Begin: From the "Read This First" page, you are invited to pause, breathe, and know you are not alone. Crystal's warm, inviting tone feels like a friend slipping you a cup of tea and saying, "I've been where you are—and I can't wait to show you how to come back home to yourself."

2. Raw Honesty About Trauma: Crystal shares the complexity of her medical PTSD, autoimmune crises, and even a brain-tumor diagnosis with refreshing transparency. When you read about her darkest nights, you realize: if she can survive—and flourish—then you can too.

3. Bridging Science and Soul: Each chapter is grounded in up-to-the-minute research on neuroplasticity, stress physiology, and more. And she doesn't stop there: she seamlessly integrates those findings into spiritual practices that bring the body's innate wisdom—and the heart's deep knowing—into harmonious dialogue, all in the name of healing.

4. Practical, Embodied Tools: Beyond theory, you'll find guided exercises, reflection questions, and movement practices that meet you wherever you are—whether you're bed-bound or dancing in your kitchen. Crystal's approach is inclusive: you are invited to rest, to write, to move, or simply to breathe. There is no hurry, no checklist—only an ever-unfolding invitation to deepen your relationship with yourself.

5. A Vision for Purpose and Empowerment: This is not a book about merely surviving chronic illness; it's about discovering—or rediscovering—your highest purpose. Crystal shows us how our physical challenges often point us toward our greatest gifts. Her own coaching practice is testimony to this: clients emerge realigned with their unique callings, armed with tools that transform pain into purpose.

As someone who has walked alongside Crystal—first online, then in person—I can attest to the power of her presence. Any reader who engages with these pages will feel her steady encouragement and unwavering belief in the human body's capacity to heal. She holds a mirror to our own resilience and invites us to step more fully into our own light.

Whether you are wrestling with physical pain, emotional overwhelm, or a sense of "What's next?", this book is your companion. It is both map and vessel: charting territory you may not yet have imagined, while holding you gently as you explore. Crystal's journey reminds us that healing is not a detour from life but its most profound expression; that trauma need not define us but can refine us; and that the path back to ourselves is, above all, a path of compassion and love.

So, take a deep breath, dear reader. Let her words wash over you like a healing tide. And know that, as you turn the page, you are not entering uncharted waters alone. Crystal is here—guide, sister, fellow traveler—ready to light the way back to the most courageous, radiant you.

XO,
Marisa Zeppieri
TEDxSpeaker, Founder of LupusChick.com 501c3, Mrs. New York,
and author of the award-winning memoir, *Chronically Fabulous*

Table of Contents

The Journey Begins: My Story of Transformation

The transformational journey can be filled with hesitancy, trepidation, and fear. I know, for me, this was the case. It wasn't until I fully embarked on the journey and moved far enough from the shore that the horizons were open in all directions, that I felt a sense of wonder, excitement, and hope. You see, some of us are lucky enough to be part of that journey as children, having those around us who welcome, inspire, and reach beyond our given thoughts and capacities for enlightenment and knowing. I envy them. I was not in those realms as a child, or even a young adult. Anything that was not formally regulated education in my world was frowned upon, made fun of, or just called malarky or a scam.

Showing emotions was considered weak, and even discussing anything that wasn't "mainstream" was crazy. When I was 11, my father took me to see a psychiatrist. My mom had left the year before to live her life outside of our family unit, and I was left to be the "woman of the house" at 10 years old. Although reflecting back, I had been taught and was doing many of those things from a younger age. Now, after years of doing the work on my mind and spirit, do I understand that my mom was seeking her own path beyond those shores that controlled her emotions and thoughts. She navigated those waters bravely without the training or the personal flotation devices that would have made the journey smoother. If I look back, it's almost like she was sent out to sea in a rowboat with no tools to navigate, where a large schooner with all the navigational technology would still have difficulty. But that is her story to tell, as my part in that comes later.

For as long as I can remember, I have been an adult. Maybe because I was treated like one, or maybe those emotions and thoughts were expected of me. I remember times when rebellion was exploding out of me with an immense urge to be free from the cages I felt consumed by. These little episodes would send my father into worry and panic, hence the psychiatrist. I remember my dad saying we were going to Pembroke Hospital to meet with someone who would fix me. Pembroke Hospital was a local mental hospital. Back in the early eighties, it was where the "crazies" were, or so I was led to believe.

We walked into the doctor's office. It was a typical professor-type office. Lots of browns, bookcases lining the walls, subdued blinds on the windows, a large, dark wood desk with a green-shaded lamp, and two upholstered chairs in front. The doctor looked studious in his suit and tie. I immediately felt judged and fearful, although my inner mind was saying, *You've got this. Don't worry. Truth always wins.* I didn't realize my inner spirit had been taking care of me all along and would continue to, even though I was not acknowledging it. We all sat down, and my father went into his concerns. I honestly don't remember a word he said. I tuned it all out. The doctor then asked to speak with me alone. My father agreed, and when he got up and looked at me, he gave me this smile of a foreboding nature, almost like, *This is all your fault, and you're going to pay for it.* I'm sure it wasn't his intent, but he was definitely happy not to have to be there.

The doctor then proceeded to ask me a bunch of questions about my life, my parents, and the situations around me. I answered with the precision of a good student, expecting the highest grades, telling my truth as I knew it. That was always required of me. "A's" were normal, and anything less was not good enough. Heaven forbid I get a "C" or tell a lie, I would be punished or have to eat soap. The doctor listened intently and seemed to understand me. He would nod his head and say, "Mmm hmmm, and what about this?" After he was done with his questions, we left. I never returned, and for a while, my father didn't say a word about it. Later in my teen years, he would tease and joke tirelessly in front of family and friends that I had to go to the shrink at the Pembroke Hospital. I was mortified, ashamed, and felt I was disappointing everyone. I had to constantly prove that I was worthy, truthful, and deserving—a very tall order for a child living with a controlling father who watched her mother grow up before her eyes alongside her every other weekend.

I did learn later as an adult from a trusted mother figure in my life, someone who helped us through those times of just being a daughter living with her dad and finding our way on our own. This couple was very close to my parents when I was growing up; they were older and had three children of their own who were older than I. They would babysit for me when my parents went out, and later when my father started dating. This woman told me that after that encounter at Pembroke Hospital with that doctor, my father continued going weekly for some time. I was floored. He never spoke of that, and when I did bring it up, the next time he poked fun at me for seeing the "shrink," he dismissed it like it was my fault he had to go.

So now you may be able to understand that the culture of personal development was something very foreign and even laughed at in my world. It meant that you were less than, weak, and not worthy. It was to be avoided at all costs. Yet, my father would always talk about horoscopes, never actually diving deep into astrology, but seeing the truth in the theory. Almost as if he yearned for more understanding and knew there was more available, but didn't want to be seen as "woo-woo."

The fact that I am now writing a so-called self-help book could be cringeworthy, but I find it truly inspiring to share my journey from that lonely sea to being at one with the earth and universe. I became curious and wanted to learn everything available to me. Sharing what I have learned and how it has helped me has become a large part of my purpose. My goal is to help you see what can be available to you if you are willing to drop your limiting beliefs and expand your consciousness into the realms beyond what you know or have been taught.

The Catalyst of Burnout and Medical PTSD

My journey toward healing began in a place of complete burnout, where my mind, body, and spirit seemed to be in constant conflict. On the outside, I appeared to be the steady captain of the ship, a typical wife, mom, and career woman who had it all together. I wore the mask of normalcy well, managing the daily tasks and responsibilities that life demanded. But beneath the surface, my mind was adrift, always strategizing, analyzing, and struggling to steer through the relentless storms that life sent my way.

The undertows of my childhood were ever-present, pulling at me with the weight of guilt and shame. My feelings were anchored in deep wounds from abandonment, the heavy responsibilities of parentification, and the unspoken trauma of sexual assault. As I moved into adulthood, new tempests arose. I found myself constantly navigating the feelings of inadequacy in a high-pressure career, the endless pursuit of success, all while enduring the insidious impact of sexual harassment in a male-dominated field. Each inappropriate comment or touch, every dismissive glance, manipulation through fear to be submissive, and the subtle yet powerful ways my worth was questioned left lasting marks. It was a constant reminder that I had to work harder, prove more, and stay vigilant just to hold my place. My mind rarely found calm waters. I lived in a state of overwhelm, where catastrophizing became my norm and survival mode my constant state.

While my mind was trapped in this endless cycle, my body bore the brunt of it. Worn down by years of complex post-trauma and the physical toll of countless anaphylactic reactions, my body was exhausted and sending urgent distress signals. I was managing a complex web of health challenges, including a spinal injury, autoimmune dysfunction, digestive disorders, chronic pain, and persistent uterine health issues. Each day felt like a new battle. I was not only grappling with the physical symptoms but also navigating a confusing and often frustrating health system. I encountered misinformation, faced dismissive medical professionals, and struggled with the effects of various medications and their side effects.

It felt as though every step forward came with a fresh obstacle, and I was constantly fighting battles on all fronts. My days were filled with doctor appointments, medical tests, and sleepless nights filled with pain and uncertainty. This is compounded by the traumatic expectations of my job and the consequences I would face if not consistently performing at top speed and with perfect execution. I was exhausted, not just physically but mentally and emotionally, as well. Amidst it all, I was still searching for something more, a path to true healing and relief that seemed to remain just out of reach.

My spirit, though overshadowed, remained a gentle whisper, longing for peace. I felt as if I were adrift at sea, surrounded by endless waves of fear and uncertainty, without a clear direction to the safety of the shore. Yet, there was a steadfast part of me that refused to give up. No matter how empty or lost I felt, I knew I needed to find a way to be present for my young children. The weight of exhaustion and despair often felt overwhelming. My inner light seemed dim, but my love for them was the anchor that kept me from completely drifting away.

Even in my darkest moments, when my body and mind were battling their own storms, my spirit held a quiet determination. I was willing to do whatever it took to find my way back to them, to be the mother and partner they needed. That love was a powerful force, a reminder that I had something to fight for. It was in this quiet chaos that I recognized the need to shift from battling the waves to learning how to navigate them with trust, curiosity, and an open heart.

My Turning Point

The ultimate fear of losing my life and leaving my children without their mother became a stark reality when I found myself in anaphylaxis again. My heart rhythms were erratic, a dangerous side effect of medications, and the inadequacies of the medical system in treating my condition. What started as a medical emergency turned into a week-long hospital stay. Lying in that hospital bed, surrounded by the cold hum of machines and a constant fear of what the many tests could reveal, I knew I could no longer put my body through this trauma. It was not sustainable. The fear of breaking my husband and shattering our family loomed larger than ever.

For as long as I could remember, I had been steering my ship through life by sheer force, charting a course that others had mapped out for me. I moved at full speed, climbing the corporate ladder, and juggling the demands of my high-stress career and family life. Even as my body began sending undeniable signals that something was wrong, I became an expert at silencing my inner voice and ignoring the whispers of my body. I pushed through every warning sign until those whispers turned into a siren I could no longer drown out.

Despite my determination to push forward, I was a mere shadow of myself. Medications numbed my mind and body, offering only a temporary escape from the pain and anxiety that seemed to follow me everywhere. My inner compass was broken, and I started to realize that the path I was on was not leading me to safety but dragging me further into a dangerous storm.

Desperate for a new direction, I began to seek other options as the traditional medical system seemed to offer only Band-Aid solutions. I found a holistic nutritionist who introduced me to ancient healing modalities and electromagnetic muscle testing, or EMT. He helped me fuel my body with foods that would not trigger my system into a shutdown. This was my first step toward truly listening to my body and understanding its needs. I also began working with a therapist who supported me through my anxiety and helped me uncover the deep layers of complex post-traumatic stress.

Learning that I was suffering from Complex Post-Traumatic Stress Disorder was both a revelation and a curse. Finally, there was a name for the chaos within me, but to me, it felt like an excuse. I had been conditioned to believe there was no excuse for suffering. In my mind, it was all my fault.

I realized that if I wanted to be there for my children and my husband, I had to take a different approach. I could no longer fight the waves. I needed to learn how to navigate them with intention, with care, and with a deep sense of compassion for myself. This was the turning point, the moment when I chose to change direction and steer my life toward healing, wholeness, and true alignment.

> *I had believed that if I just did more and worked harder, I would finally prove that I was enough.*

The Shift from Doing to Being

The shift that fueled my healing journey into motion began when I realized that my constant doing, achieving, and striving were not leading me toward peace or fulfillment. I had believed that if I just did more and worked harder, I would finally prove that I was enough. But the more I pushed, the further I drifted from myself. My mind was always busy, my body was always exhausted, and my spirit felt like an impostor beneath the noise of life.

I needed a different approach. I needed to shift from constantly doing and proving to simply being. From living in a state of survival and urgency to actually embracing and enjoying my life. This was not an overnight change but a gradual unveiling of old beliefs and the rebuilding of new, nurturing my truths.

One of the most powerful practices that helped me shift was ballroom dancing. It combined the precision of the mind, the control and movement of my body, and the energy and feelings in my spirit. When I danced, I was free. I had never experienced a sense of freedom. It became my recipe, a practice of being fully present in my body and allowing myself to move with feeling and intention along with the music. Each step, each movement, was a chance to express my inner world, an opportunity to let my feelings flow in a way that words never could.

Through storytelling with dance, I began to cultivate a true sense of self-love and compassion. It helped me create a sacred space where I could connect with my spirit and listen to what it needed. Dancing was more than just movement for me. It was an invitation to be present with myself, to honor my journey, and to find joy in the simplicity of being seen for who I truly am. This became a cornerstone of my healing, a reminder that I could find balance and harmony not by doing more, but by allowing myself to be in the moment and by letting myself be vulnerable to the world.

Yet, even as I felt the benefits of this healing through self-acceptance, Lupus reared its ugly head. It felt like a betrayal, as if my body was telling me that I was not enough. I had been focusing on my mind through therapy, although the process felt somewhat slow and unsteady. I was nurturing my body with exercise and proper nutrition, doing all the "right" things. But despite it all, something was missing. My body was holding on to pain and illness, showing me that there was a deeper layer I had not allowed myself to explore.

It became clear that healing was not just about my mind or my body. It was about something more. It was about connecting with my spirit and finding what truly aligned with my inner truth. This realization opened another door in my healing journey, showing me that true healing meant listening not just with my mind or my body but with my whole being. I needed to find harmony within the sea of my life, allowing myself to move with the currents of my past, present, and future, rather than constantly battling against them.

Finding Harmony in Traditional, Modern, and Spiritual Healing Methods

Exploring the balance of traditional, modern, and spiritual healing practices transformed my perspective in profound ways. My healing journey began with a desperate need to find relief from the physical and emotional storms that were consuming my life. When I was battling Lupus, it felt as if every step forward was met with a new obstacle. Many say autoimmune conditions are the body attacking itself. That definition alone leads to blame and shame directed at your body. I hated what was happening, and my body became the target of that blame. Traditional medicine provided some temporary relief, but it often felt like just another step on their ladder of treatment, leading only to a total system breakdown. "This is incurable," they said. "There is no solution." I was managing some symptoms while gaining others through side effects, but I was not finding true healing.

For a long time, I found myself slipping into a victim mentality. The weight of my circumstances felt heavy, and it became easy to focus on what was happening to me, what I was no longer able to do, and what I had to avoid to slow the progression of my illness. It was easy to listen to the doctors and read the information they provided, which often led me down a whirlpool of despair. My mind was filled with thoughts of helplessness, and my spirit felt disconnected. Questions like *Was I going to become disabled?* and *What would the rest of my life look like?* became constant companions.

This mindset created a cycle where my body mirrored my inner world, amplifying my physical symptoms and keeping me stuck in a state of illness. Recognizing this pattern was a pivotal moment. I began to see how my mind and spirit were directly influencing my body's ability to heal.

I began to open the door to healing beyond just the traditional physical level. I continued working with the holistic nutritionist who guided me in nourishing my body with foods that promoted healing instead of harm, and removing those that cause inflammation. I learned about ancient practices like meditation, Ayurveda, and energy work, which allowed me to connect with my spirit and calm my mind. Therapy helped me uncover the deep layers of complex post-traumatic stress that had woven themselves into my body's reactions and my mind's patterns. I started to understand how my unresolved traumas were manifesting as physical illness, and this awareness was a crucial step toward healing.

The shift from a victim mindset to a place of empowerment was not easy, but it was necessary to begin the process of true healing. I shifted from asking, *Why is this happening to me?* to *What is my body trying to tell me?* which allowed me to see my body not as a villain that had betrayed me but as an ally and partner, guiding me toward what I truly needed to heal. I also began to recognize how my circumstances, including being a victim of toxic people and enduring sexual harassment, were additional fuel for the illness in my body. Our emotions and thoughts rule our body. When I started listening to my body with curiosity and approaching my spirit with compassion, true healing began.

When the unexpected diagnosis of a brain tumor came, it initially felt like another storm on the horizon. I found myself questioning my body yet again. Although, this time, I was not caught off guard. I had built a foundation through years of learning to listen to my body, quiet my mind, and strengthen my spirit. Instead of being consumed by fear, I now knew this was just the product of all the traumas in my body. It had to reside somewhere, and I had refused to allow it the light of day for so long. I leaned into the practices that had carried me through Lupus. I honored my voice, set and held my boundaries, questioned everything I had been conditioned to know and be, and allowed my traumas to be the mast that had built the ship. I was the captain.

Integrating traditional, modern, and spiritual healing practices did more than prepare me for the physical, mental, and emotional challenges of brain surgery. It fortified my spirit. I approached this experience not as a victim of circumstance but as an active participant in my own healing. I discovered that true healing was not just about eradicating illness but about finding a deep, unwavering trust in my own strength and the wisdom of my mind, body, and spirit working together as one. When I found my lighthouse of meditation, it brought me calm, a deeper connection to spirituality and meaning, and a newfound sense of purpose.

Finding Purpose in the Journey

My journey through healing did more than restore my mind, body, and spirit. It revealed my purpose. As I navigated my own storms, I began to see that my experiences were not just a story of survival but a guide for others. Each challenge I faced, from CPTSD to anaphylaxis to Lupus and the brain tumor, from emotional trauma to spiritual awakening, became a lantern lighting the way for those still lost in the fog and not truly living their authentic life.

So many of us move through life carrying the expectations of others, like a tiny tugboat pushing a massive container ship through a narrow channel. Maybe the tugboat wants to pull instead of push. More likely, she longs to be free to roam the waters beyond the channel, to find her own way.

I realized that the sea I had once feared held the potential to set me free. By learning to read the tides of my emotions, to trust my inner compass, and to steer my own course, I transformed my life from merely surviving to genuinely thriving. I shifted from trudging through the life expected of me to fully embracing my divine self. This transformation planted the seeds for Mission Me 2.0. I knew that my journey to find a life filled with purpose, balance, and joy was meant to serve as a guide for others to do the same.

Coaching became the vessel through which I could share what I had learned. It allowed me to offer support, guidance, and a safe harbor for those ready to embark on their own journeys. I integrated all the modalities that helped me along the way. Holistic nutrition, positive psychology, solution-focused brief therapy, meditation, energy healing, setting boundaries, and the profound experience of truly being seen and heard. More importantly, finding validation and solace in your truths, and seeing the light that guides you back to you. My purpose became crystal clear. I wanted to empower others to listen to their bodies, connect with their spirits, and navigate life with intention and clarity. Mission Me 2.0 was born from this calling, a map for those seeking to explore the depths of their potential and move confidently toward the life they truly desire. Are you ready for your 2.0?

Through coaching, I found a way to transform my past pain into a source of light. It is a privilege to hold space for others as they navigate their own paths, helping them turn the unknown into an adventure of self-discovery and fulfillment. Each person I work with becomes a reminder of the incredible strength we all possess and the profound healing that can happen when we choose to embrace our journey with an open mind and a loving heart.

The Truth About Healing and Personal Growth

Healing isn't about fixing yourself. It's about returning to who you've always been. True transformation isn't about fixing what is broken but rather about peeling away the layers that have been built up over time. Stress, trauma, and limiting beliefs fail to reveal your authentic self. We never really return to our childhood innocence, but we can return to that curiosity and inquisitive nature. Using your intuition and creative imagination, you can ignite that fire within. The human body is an immense technical miracle. Many forget that the brain is an organ within that miracle, and your spirit resides in the heart, nervous system, and mind, and extends all around you, connecting you to the amazing web of the universe. If you are brave enough to venture out beyond the known territory, those uncharted waters are where you will find yourself again. Questioning everything you know with the curiosity and wonder of your inner child fuels the journey of the mind. Exploring with wonder and excitement for what lies ahead is the map to the treasure of your true spirit.

Healing isn't about fixing yourself. It's about returning to who you've always been.

This book is your guide back to you. A new journey through your mind, body, and spirit. Reuniting yourself with your true intentions, core beliefs, and purpose. Using your past challenges to find your superpowers and unlimited resources, we embark on discovering the authentic you. Releasing the expectations holding you back from your true self—those of society, family, and friends that have built up over time and created the many masks and characters we've become in our quest to be accepted and loved. Love starts in you. With your mind, body, and spirit. It cannot exist unlimited without that bond.

I invite you to embark on this journey with me, to step away from the familiar shores of what you know, and venture into the open waters of what is truly possible. Whether you find yourself navigating the rough seas of burnout, facing health challenges, or simply yearning for a new direction, Mission Me 2.0 offers more than inspiration. It is a guide that combines science, practical tools, and a holistic approach to healing to create real and lasting change.

Mission Me 2.0 offers a pathway to find clarity where there is confusion, to cultivate courage where there is fear, and to experience healing where there is hurt. It includes insights into how our thoughts and emotions influence our physical health, how to use mindfulness to reduce stress, and how small shifts in mindset and lifestyle can lead to profound transformation. You will explore new perspectives, uncover your inner resilience, and gain a deeper understanding of yourself and your mind-body-spirit connection.

The first step in this journey is to pause. Take a moment to breathe, check in with yourself, and notice what you are feeling right now. This small act of mindfulness is not just a moment of stillness but an opportunity to connect with your internal world. Research shows that even brief pauses can shift your brain from a reactive state to a more reflective and responsive one. It creates space for awareness, where true change begins.

I encourage you to reflect on two pivotal questions:

When in your life have you felt the most aligned?

_____

_____

_____

_____

_____

When have you felt the most lost?

_____

_____

_____

_____

_____

These reflections are not about judgment. This is about gathering insight into your internal narrative and connecting with your true self. This is the starting point of uncovering your patterns, beliefs, and experiences that have shaped your journey so far. When I first asked myself these questions, I was truly surprised by what came up. It was not the big life events you'd expect. It was more the quiet moments of peace by myself and the deep pulls of discomfort and confusion that showed me where my true path to healing lay. As you read this book, I encourage you to take moments to pause, breathe, and reflect. Let these moments of stillness be the foundation upon which you build your journey toward clarity, healing, and fulfillment.

Are you ready to begin your own Mission Me 2.0? I am honored to walk beside you on this journey, offering guidance, support, and the tools to help you navigate your unique path forward. The answers you seek are already within you. Let this book be the lighthouse that helps you find your way back to yourself, with both the wisdom of ancient practices and the strength of modern science lighting the way.

CHAPTER 1

The Mission Me 2.0 Framework: Science & Soul of Transformation

There are many times in our lives when we feel disconnected, stagnant, or stuck—when we're just going through the motions: morning routine, workday, dinner, evening routine, sleep. Repeat. Again and again. I know when I was in the thick of being a mom, wife, and career woman, this was my life. I had the occasional bouts of awareness and happiness, usually on the weekends with Sunday family dinners or get-togethers with friends. But the majority of my life was the same record on repeat. Angst of dealing with the office and its toxic culture, and staying up late after the kids were in bed to get stuff done. Is this really the life we want to live?

I loved being a mom, and the little treasures that would come up, but I was mostly hearing about them from their grandmother or other caregivers because I was so in the grind. It was only when I was dealing with health issues that I realized how disconnected I was from everything around me. I was always exhausted and wondering when I would finally feel rested and really enjoy being a mom. I would have those moments, usually on weekends or holidays, where I would get to build Legos with my son, dance around with my daughter, or be in the garden with them, picking vegetables or cooking something special.

When we feel lost and afloat, our brain likes to protect us from that uncertainty. We get busy, do more, and shove the thoughts away. We cannot look incapable or weak. We pull up our bootstraps and just go forward. Like those times when we're young and experience emotions based on our circumstances, and an authority figure tells us not to cry, or they'll "give you something to cry about." You're dismissed as emotional or maybe even delusional—especially as a woman in a corporate environment where if you show emotions or stand up for yourself, you're seen as a bitch. This stress of binding our emotions for the sake of others' judgments for safety leads us into a state of disconnect. Numbness. We're not truly being ourselves; we're not authentic. We hide, cover up, and become something we feel is safe. This is where we are living in the fight, flight, or freeze state of survival. It becomes a constant burden of stress on our mind, spirit, and even our body.

Why You Might Feel Disconnected (And Why It's Not Your Fault)

We live in a world that rewards performance more than presence. From an early age, we're taught to produce, to keep going, to manage our emotions quietly, and meet expectations without complaint. We learn to push past exhaustion. To dismiss the whispers from our bodies. To keep showing up, even when what we're showing up for doesn't feel true. Somewhere along the way, we start measuring our value by how well we keep it all together. We override exhaustion, silence our needs, and wear our productivity like a badge.

Eventually, this becomes a rhythm we don't even question. The full calendar. The late-night scroll. The tight shoulders. The stress we normalize and the silence we mistake for strength. We learn to call this survival, and we convince ourselves it's just what life is. This pattern catches up to us. Maybe your body breaks down. Maybe you feel a numbness that won't lift. Maybe you wake up one day and realize you don't even recognize your own life anymore. You're not broken for feeling this way. You're human.

Our culture rarely teaches us how to rest, how to listen, or how to feel safe in stillness. And it almost never teaches us how to reconnect with the wisdom of the body or the truth of our spirit. So we survive. We adapt. We check the boxes and keep going. But deep down, something aches. Something longs for realignment. That ache? It's not a flaw. It's a guide. It's the invitation.

Suddenly, the mask we've been wearing doesn't fit the same way. That moment is disorienting, and we question it. We dismiss it. Sometimes, a few times. It comes back, though, because it's sacred. That's when we begin to feel the truth beneath the autopilot. That's when the part of us that's been waiting to be heard begins to speak.

If you're reading this and nodding or feeling something stir, know this: nothing is wrong with you. Disconnection is not a flaw. It's a response. It's the body's way of saying, *I've been carrying too much for too long.* You don't need to push harder. You don't need to prove anything. You don't need to be perfect to begin.

You're already here. And that's enough.

How Science and Spirituality Work Together for Real Transformation

Throughout my own healing, I realized something that changed everything: true transformation happens when science and spirituality stop competing and start collaborating. When I paired neurological rewiring with grounding practices like meditation and energy work, the shifts I experienced didn't just feel good in the moment, they began to last. The science helped me understand what was happening in my brain. The spirituality reminded me I wasn't broken—I was evolving.

For example, I began practicing mindfulness alongside somatic release. Mindfulness calmed my nervous system and helped me become aware of what I was feeling in the moment, rather than reacting automatically. Somatic release is a body-based approach that helps process and release stored emotions and tension through movement, breath, and sensation. It allowed my body to let go of what it had been holding and gave my spirit permission to speak again. The science behind these practices confirmed what I was feeling. My brain was calming the amygdala, the part responsible for fear and stress, and my nervous system was beginning to regulate and heal.

The spiritual practice taught me to trust myself again. To see pain as a message, not a punishment. The more I honored both, the more integrated I felt. My healing no longer lived in separate compartments. It became a living rhythm. This marriage of modalities became a cornerstone of my healing. When we bridge the gap between these two worlds, we access something deeper: alignment. This is where alignment begins. Not just a mindset shift, but a soul shift. The kind of change that isn't about fixing anything. It's about remembering who you are underneath the noise.

The Mind-Body-Spirit Connection: Why Mindset Alone Isn't Enough

If mindset were enough, I would've healed years earlier. I spent so long trying to "think" my way to health. Telling myself I was strong and trying to stay positive. I put on the mask and smiled through the pain. I read the books and repeated the affirmations. And still, I was exhausted. But no amount of positive thinking could override what my body was holding on to. The inflammation, the anxiety, the burnout, they weren't just symptoms. They were messages. Signals from a body that had been whispering for years, and eventually started to scream. My spirit was screaming: *you're off course*. What I didn't understand back then is that you can't outthink your body. You can't spiritually bypass your pain.

It wasn't until I worked with all of me—my thoughts, my cells, my spirit—that healing began to take root. I began nourishing my body with anti-inflammatory foods. I practiced yoga and breathwork to release stuck energy. When I nourished my body, I calmed my mind. I created boundaries and asked hard questions. I embraced silence, stillness, and curiosity. When I honored my emotions, I stopped needing to control everything around me. When I reconnected with my spirit, I remembered I wasn't here to perform. I was here to live.

Mindset is only part of the equation. We need to feel it in our bodies. We need to believe it in our bones. We need to reconnect to the deep inner knowing that says, *You already have everything you need, so let's clear the path back to it.*

Mindset is only part of the equation. We need to feel it in our bodies. We need to believe it in our bones.

What It Means to Come Back to You

Coming back to yourself doesn't usually arrive with a lightning bolt or some perfectly timed breakthrough. Sometimes it's subtle, almost imperceptible. A moment when your body finally exhales after holding tension you didn't even realize was there. A morning when you wake up and, for once, don't feel the weight of dread pressing down on your chest. A feeling that rises when you're in the garden with your hands in the dirt, or when you're cooking something from memory instead of following a recipe. No performance. Just presence.

You may not have words for it yet. That's okay. You don't need a roadmap. Just a willingness to listen for the moments when you feel like *you* again. Sometimes that return comes quietly, like in the car when a song reminds you of who you were before life got heavy. Sometimes it arrives in hard moments, like when your body says *enough* and you finally stop pushing. When you feel something stir that you forgot you even had inside you.

Other times, the return feels like grief, like realizing how far you've drifted from the version of yourself you used to know. The one who used to dream or laugh without needing to be productive, or sit still without guilt. It can be painful to notice the gap. But that noticing is powerful. Because it means you're already coming home. Coming back to yourself isn't a task to complete. It's a rhythm to remember.

It's not about fixing what's broken. It's about softening what's been hardened. Making space for what's true. Asking better questions, not chasing better answers. It's realizing that healing doesn't always look like progress. Sometimes it looks like stillness. Sometimes it looks like walking away. Sometimes it looks like finally letting someone see what you've been hiding.

For me, it began in stolen moments: building Legos with my son when I didn't have a million other things demanding my attention, dancing in the kitchen with my daughter, sitting on the porch, tea in hand, not doing anything "productive" and letting that be enough.

That feeling, that spark of truth or warmth or breath, is what this book is here to nurture. This book isn't going to give you a blueprint for becoming someone new. It's going to help you notice what already feels like home in your body, in your breath, in your truth. We won't chase transformation. We'll return to it. Together.

What to Expect in the Book: A Blend of Research, Practical Tools, Personal Insights, and Guided Exercises

This book is not meant to sit on a shelf. It's meant to walk with you. This is not just a book. It's a guide. A companion. A mirror to help you remember who you truly are.

You'll find research here, the kind that helps you understand why your nervous system is in survival mode, or why you shut down when you're overwhelmed. You'll also find practices— not rigid routines, but rhythms that meet you where you are.

You'll hear stories—mine, and echoes of others—not to tell you what to do, but to remind you that you are not alone. This book is for the part of you that's tired of living on autopilot. The part that knows you're meant for more than stress management and survival. The part that's already waking up, even if the next step feels unclear.

Each chapter is woven with the following:

- **Personal stories** that prove healing is not linear, but possible, so your heart can soften, and you know you are not alone on this journey.

- **Scientific insights** that explain why your stress, anxiety, or burnout aren't "all in your head," so your mind can understand this path is safe and proven.

- **Spiritual tools and practices** to reconnect with yourself, your truth, and your purpose, so your body can respond and connect fully with your heart and mind.

- **Guided exercises** to move from confusion to clarity, and from surviving to thriving.

- **Space**, so your spirit can breathe and awaken to your true self.

Every chapter builds upon the last. Each one offers a piece of the puzzle until you begin to see yourself, whole and clear. This isn't about becoming someone else. It's about reclaiming what you were always meant to be: *whole, clear, and aligned.*

This book is grounded in a balanced integration of mind, body, and spirit practices, drawing on evidence-based methods from psychology and neuroscience, along with holistic approaches like mindfulness, nutrition, and energy healing. Through these combined modalities, Mission Me 2.0 offers a comprehensive path to healing and personal growth. You will learn how to listen to your body, calm your mind, and connect with your spirit through evidence-based methods that blend traditional wisdom with modern science. I share practices and exercises that support healing, cultivate self-awareness, and empower you to take tangible steps toward the life you truly deserve.

How to Use This Book (and What Not to Expect)

This isn't the kind of book you need to race through or finish in one sitting. It's not for you to power through with a highlighter and a deadline. It's not meant to be consumed in one sitting or ticked off a list like a task to be completed. It's not about checking boxes or achieving healing on a timeline. There's no gold star waiting for you at the end. No quiz to prove you did it right. This is an invitation to be with yourself in a different way, slower, softer, and more curious than you've probably been taught to be. It's meant to walk with you.

Some books are written to give you answers. This one is here to help you *live* your questions. Some days, you may read a few paragraphs and feel full. Other days, you may find yourself underlining every line in a chapter. You may find yourself lingering in a single paragraph for days, turning a sentence over in your mind like a smooth stone in your pocket. You might read an entire chapter in one afternoon, or come back to the same page more than once, hearing something different each time. There's no wrong pace. Some sections might ask more of you than others. Some may simply confirm what you've already started to feel. That's part of the rhythm. That's part of your return. That's not just okay, that's how this book was designed to be used.

There is no "finish line" here. No test at the end. No final breakthrough moment that promises a forever fix. Healing isn't a checklist. It's a cycle of remembering. And this book is a space to remember who you are slowly, honestly, and in your own time.

If you begin a chapter and feel resistance, that's part of the process. If you feel emotional and don't know why, that's part of it, too. If you need to pause and put the book down to let something settle in your body, do that. Your nervous system knows when it's time to pause. Your spirit knows when it needs space.

There may be times when the material resonates immediately, and others when you feel unsure or uncomfortable. That's not a sign to skip ahead or shut down, it's a sign that something is shifting. The tools in this book are here to help you notice, not force. To support, not direct. They're invitations, not obligations.

> Healing isn't a checklist. It's a cycle of remembering.

If all you do is read and gently reflect, that's enough. If you feel called to write, to move, to speak, or to share, that's welcome, too. But there's no one right way to move through this experience. No perfect reader to become. You don't have to start over every time you fall back into old patterns. You don't have to have all the answers to keep going. This isn't a one-way road, it's a spiral. Each chapter brings you deeper into something you already hold within you.

You will not be asked to push harder. You will not be asked to override your truth. You will never be told that your worth is something to earn. Instead, you'll be invited to explore through story, through science, and through spirit what it might feel like to live in alignment with the person you've always been beneath the noise.

This book won't fix you because you are not broken. But it will hold space for your process. It will offer tools, stories, science, and soul so you can start to see yourself more clearly. It will help you notice the quiet patterns that have shaped your life and the quiet power you've had all along to shift them.

Let it be a guide, not a rulebook. A companion, not a checklist. A place to come home to when the world feels loud or your own voice gets hard to hear. So bring your journal. Bring your questions. Bring your whole self, even the parts that feel tired, unsure, or messy.

However you move through it, just keep returning. You don't need to be ready, you just need to be willing. That's the work. That's the path. That's the journey of coming back to *you*.

Action Step: Set an Intention — What Do You Want to Gain from This Journey?

Before we go any further, this might be a good place to pause. You've already taken the first step just by opening these pages, by being curious enough to wonder what it might feel like to come back to yourself in a deeper way. This journey we're about to take together isn't something to rush. It isn't something to fix. It's something to feel. To notice. To hold.

Maybe this is the first time in a long time you've done that and slowed down long enough to ask yourself what you really need. If you feel comfortable, you might let your eyes soften or close. Maybe you feel the weight of your body wherever you're sitting, the way your chest rises and falls. You might feel the breath settle a little deeper into your belly, or your shoulders shift just enough to remind you you're allowed to let go.

This is a moment for you. Just you. No one else to answer to. No performance required. And in this space, with no pressure, no right way, you might begin to wonder: what is it I'm really hoping to receive from this journey?

It's not the checklist answer. Not the one someone else might expect from you. But the answer that lives deeper than that. The one that doesn't need to be said aloud to be true. It might come as a word or a sensation. It might come as a quiet whisper of a need that's been waiting for permission to speak.

You may notice a longing for clarity. Or peace. Or the courage to choose yourself without guilt. Maybe it's as simple as wanting to feel a little more like *you* again. Or maybe you don't know yet, and that's okay, too. Whatever rises here, let it come. Let it be messy. Let it be quiet. Let it be real. You might write it down if that feels right. Not for the sake of documentation, but as a way to gently mark this beginning. You don't have to carve it in stone. You're allowed to change your mind. You're allowed to grow as you go.

This book won't ask you to become anyone new. It will simply invite you to return to the version of you that has always been here, just waiting to be remembered.

Closing Reflection: An Invitation to Choose You

There was a time in my life when everything looked fine from the outside. I was doing all the things: career woman, mother, wife, multitasker, achiever. My days ran like clockwork: the morning routine, the commute, the office chaos, the late nights after the kids were in bed, trying to catch up on everything I didn't get to. Weekdays were a blur. Weekends were when I felt glimmers of myself. Sunday dinners, Lego towers with my son, dancing barefoot in the kitchen with my daughter, pulling vegetables from the garden with dirt still under my nails. Little flashes of presence. And then Monday would start all over again.

I told myself that was enough. That the joy in the margins would carry me through. But I was exhausted. My body was tired. My mind was overworked. And somewhere along the way, my spirit had become so quiet I couldn't hear it anymore. What I didn't realize then was that I was holding up a life that no longer fit. I wasn't broken. But I was out of alignment. I had learned how to survive. I hadn't yet learned how to *choose* myself.

Maybe no one ever told you that it's okay to put yourself first. Not in a way that feels selfish or loud or demanding, but in a way that feels like a quiet return. A steady breath. A hand resting on your heart when the world gets too loud. You've likely spent so much of your life focused on what needs to be done. On who needs you. On how to be everything for everyone. Somewhere along the way, you learned how to show up—for work, for family, for expectations. But maybe not always for yourself.

Not because you didn't want to. But because there was never space. Or permission. Or time. This journey is about changing that. That's why this chapter doesn't end with an action item or a checklist. It ends with a return. A moment to ask: *What if I didn't have to wait until the next crisis to come back to myself?*

Choosing yourself doesn't mean leaving your family behind or walking away from your responsibilities. It means showing up to your life. Your *real* life. With presence. With curiosity. With compassion for the parts of you that are still healing from years of doing what you thought you had to. Choosing yourself doesn't mean abandoning others. It means remembering you were never meant to disappear in the first place. It means honoring the part of you that has been quietly waiting for your own attention.

That part may feel small at first. Tired. Hesitant. You don't need to rush it. You don't need to know exactly what it wants yet. Just notice that it's still there. That *you're* still there, underneath it all. That version of you, the one who kept going, kept giving, and kept showing up even when it was empty, was trying her best. She believed that rest would come later. That joy could wait.

But the truth is, we don't have to earn our peace. We don't have to prove our worth before we come home to ourselves. As you close these first pages, you might not feel ready. That's okay. Most of us don't feel ready for the deep work when we begin. But there's something more important than being ready. Let this moment be your soft beginning.

Being willing.

Willing to pause. Willing to listen. Willing to believe there's more waiting for you than the life you've been taught to endure. So, before you turn the page, let this moment be your first yes. No declarations. No pressure. Just a quiet yes.

Yes to paying attention. Yes to coming back. Yes to the life that still lives beneath the noise. Yes to slowing down. Yes to asking different questions. Yes to making room for yourself. Not someday, but *NOW*.

You are not here to perform wellness. You are here to remember who you are. Because this journey isn't about becoming a better version of you. It's about coming back to the one who's always been there.

And when you're ready, we'll turn the page together.

PHASE 1

Laying the Foundation: Awareness & Intention

CHAPTER 2

Awakening to Your Truth: Understanding Where You Are

Personal Story: A Moment in My Journey When I Realized I Was Misaligned

One evening, after a long, stressful day at work, my husband and I came home together. We used to work together, which meant we carried that stress home with us every day. My kids were teenagers at the time, and they had certain chores they were supposed to do after school before we got home. Most days, we'd walk in the door to find them goofing off with the chores left undone. We were already exhausted and tense from the day, and the first thing out of my mouth would be, "Why didn't you get that done? What were you doing all day?" It wasn't just frustration; it was years of conditioning surfacing, pushing me to expect things to be done a certain way. The way I was raised.

I grew up with a very strict father. My mom had left when I was young, so all the chores and expectations landed on me. And if I didn't get them done, the consequences were severe. I swore I wouldn't be that kind of parent. I didn't want my kids to feel the way I did. So, I tried to be less strict, less demanding. Their chores were small, manageable. Empty the dishwasher, load dishes from breakfast, and scoop the cat box. I think that's why it made me so angry when they weren't done. It felt like we weren't asking for a lot.

But that night, my daughter called me out. She said, "Why is it that all you do when you come home is complain that we didn't get anything done? You don't even say hi. You don't ask how our day was. You just yell at us about the chores." Hearing that from my daughter made me stop in my tracks. Her words took me back to my own childhood and reminded me of my own feelings at her age and younger. Of the heaviness I felt from having to do everything on my own, of the frustration and resentment of never feeling like I could do enough. And suddenly, I saw that I was repeating the same pattern. Even though I had tried to lighten the load, I was still reacting the same way my father did.

I didn't want to be that parent. I didn't want them to think I only saw them for what they "got done" or the contribution they made at home. It made me realize how far outside of myself I had drifted. I was bringing all the stress from my toxic work environment home and turning it against the people I loved most. So, I started to change. I began letting go of that automatic reaction and focusing on how I wanted my kids to feel. I wanted to be a parent who asked how their day was. Who really listened to them. Who chose compassion over criticism. It wasn't perfect, but it was a turning point.

The Neuroscience of Self-Awareness—Why We Repeat Patterns and How the Brain Resists Change

When I came home after a long, toxic workday, my reactions to my kids were automatic. Snapping at them about undone chores wasn't a conscious choice; it was a pattern. One that had developed over years of stress and unmet expectations, driven by a deep-seated belief that productivity and achievement were the most important markers of success. This conditioning was reinforced by my upbringing, where chores were expected and completed out of fear of punishment rather than a sense of cooperation or connection.

The science behind these habitual reactions is rooted in neuroplasticity, the brain's remarkable ability to rewire itself based on repeated thought patterns and behaviors. Neuroscientists like Dr. Michael Merzenich and Dr. Norman Doidge have demonstrated that our brains form strong neural pathways around habitual behaviors and beliefs, making change difficult (2007).

Dr. Michael Merzenich has been a pioneer in the study of cortical plasticity. His work shows that the brain physically rewires itself through repetition, which means that habits, both helpful and harmful, are deeply embedded through repeated activation of the same neural pathways (2013). The more you react in a certain way, the stronger that neural connection becomes. The more I responded to my kids with frustration and criticism, the stronger those neural pathways became. It's like forging a path through a forest; the more you walk the same route, the clearer and more defined it becomes. Do you ever notice when you're driving or walking somewhere you do all the time that when you get there, you don't remember the journey? You were on autopilot, a conditioned response embedded in your neural pathways.

Understanding how these patterns form is the first step. Awareness engages the prefrontal cortex, the part of the brain responsible for decision-making, emotional regulation, and conscious thought. When I realized I was reacting to my children out of habit rather than intention, I activated this part of my brain, creating an opportunity to break the cycle and choose a different response. This awareness allowed me to begin the process of rewiring my brain through intentional action.

The moment you see the pattern, you can choose to do something different. When I actively engaged in the process of awareness by choosing different responses to my children, I was rewiring my brain. Each time I responded with curiosity instead of criticism, I strengthened the neural circuits supporting compassionate communication. I started to ask questions about their day at school—things like: "What was good? What sucked? What did they have on their plate for the evening?" My body responded positively to these shifts. Reduced stress, tension, and frustration showed me that my nervous system was moving away from fight or flight and toward relaxation and healing. I no longer worried about any mess at home. I would help when they had heavy schoolwork loads. I didn't want to send my kids into fight or flight. Over time, this contributed to a more harmonious home environment. Spiritually, neuroplasticity is about growth and evolution. By choosing a different response, I was aligning more deeply with my authentic self, instead of the conditioned one. My intuition guided me toward greater patience and understanding, helping to nurture a better relationship built on love and acceptance.

The moment you see the pattern, you can choose to do something different.

Repeated stress responses also take a physical toll. The sympathetic nervous system activates in fight-or-flight mode when faced with perceived threats. In my case, the stress from work would carry over into my interactions at home, creating physical symptoms like tightness in my chest, headaches, and fatigue. My body was conditioned to react defensively because my brain had established a pattern of associating stress with confrontation. Spiritually, breaking free from these patterns was about reconnecting with my authentic self. It required me to go beyond automatic reactions and tune into a deeper truth. One rooted in love, compassion, and the desire to nurture my children rather than control them.

The beauty of the brain's neuroplasticity is that it's never too late to change. Dr. Merzenich's research highlights that repeated behaviors can physically rewire the brain, supporting long-term change. When I became aware of my reaction patterns, I began to consciously choose different responses. Every time I decided to approach my children with curiosity and compassion rather than frustration, I was laying down new neural pathways. From a scientific perspective, neuroplasticity explains why intentional thought patterns and behaviors can break self-sabotaging cycles. The brain's ability to rewire itself means that transformation is not only possible but inevitable when approached with consistency and dedication. Recognizing old patterns and actively choosing new responses helps build the neural networks that support change.

Every positive interaction with my children reinforced new pathways focused on empathy and connection rather than criticism and control. As I rewired my mind, my body followed. The stress response lessened, physical symptoms like tension and headaches diminished, and I began to feel more relaxed and present with my family. From a spiritual standpoint, this was about releasing old conditioning and embracing my true purpose as a compassionate, present, and loving parent. The transformation wasn't just mental; it was a soul-level shift toward authenticity.

Another key player in breaking habitual patterns is the Reticular Activating System, or RAS. Located in the brainstem, the RAS acts as a filter, deciding which information is important and worth focusing on. It's the reason why, once you decide to buy a certain car, you suddenly see that car everywhere. The RAS prioritizes what you focus on and helps bring it to the forefront of your awareness. If I said, "Wow, look at that pink elephant!" you automatically see a pink elephant in your mind.

Dr. Shad Helmstetter has demonstrated how the RAS works as the brain's gatekeeper (1986). When I focused on the negative, what my kids hadn't done or how their behavior failed to meet my expectations, my RAS filtered my experiences to support those perceptions. I was primed to notice what was wrong, rather than what was right. Research also shows that visualization, affirmations, and setting intentions help retrain the RAS to focus on desired outcomes rather than negative patterns.

By choosing to approach my children with empathy and genuine curiosity, I began to reprogram my brain's filter, allowing me to see opportunities for connection rather than conflict. Setting new intentions and visualizing positive interactions with my children helped me redirect my brain's filter. By focusing on moments of connection rather than confrontation, I gradually rewired my RAS to prioritize positive experiences.

Self-awareness is the first step to transformation.

As my mindset shifted, my body responded with calmness. Instead of feeling tense and reactive, I began to feel at ease and more present during interactions with my children. Spiritually, this was about shifting from a mindset of fear and control to one of love and acceptance. The RAS became a tool for aligning my thoughts and actions with my higher self, creating a more harmonious and fulfilling relationship with my children.

Self-awareness is the first step to transformation. Neuroscientists have shown that when you become aware of a pattern or reaction, you activate the prefrontal cortex, the part of the brain responsible for decision-making, emotional regulation, and conscious thought. This awareness is what allows you to interrupt automatic behaviors and choose a different response.

For example, if you come home expecting your kids to have slacked off, your brain will immediately notice anything that confirms this belief. The RAS will highlight the dirty dishes or uncompleted chores, rather than recognizing any positive aspects of the situation. When you shift your focus to something more positive or intentionally set a new intention, the RAS begins to filter for evidence of what you want to see instead. Neuroscientists have demonstrated that the brain and body are deeply interconnected. Emotions, especially those rooted in conditioned beliefs, manifest physically.

Chronic stress and unresolved emotional patterns can manifest as headaches, muscle tension, or fatigue. This supports the realization that habitual behaviors are stored not only in the brain but also in the body. When you bring awareness to these sensations and patterns, you can begin to change them. Awareness activates the prefrontal cortex, allowing you to make conscious choices rather than reacting from conditioned patterns. This process is deeply connected to your intuition and higher self.

When my daughter spoke up and voiced her frustration, my body reacted before my mind even had a chance to process her words. The flush of heat, the clenching in my chest, all of it was my body's way of signaling that something was out of alignment. My RAS had been conditioned to notice what was wrong, chores left undone, expectations unmet, rather than seeing the underlying need for connection and understanding. This automatic response was rooted in my own childhood experiences, where discipline and productivity were prioritized over emotional connection.

But the moment I became aware of the pattern, I activated the prefrontal cortex. I was able to step outside the automatic reaction and consciously choose a different response. This awareness allowed me to begin rewiring my brain, shifting from old patterns of anger and frustration to new patterns of compassion and authenticity.

Questions for Reflection:

What patterns do you notice in your automatic reactions to stress or frustration?

_____

_____

_____

How does your body signal when something is out of alignment?

_____

_____

_____

_____

When you bring awareness to these patterns, what new possibilities open up for you?

_____

_____

_____

Recognizing the Gap Between Who You Are Versus Who You Think You Should Be

Many of us carry an internal image of who we believe we _should_ be, and this often creates a disconnect between our true selves and the version of ourselves that we feel obligated to present to the world. This gap is shaped by three main influences.

1. **Childhood conditioning:** expectations from parents, teachers, or cultural norms deeply influence how we perceive success and self-worth. If you were raised to believe that your value is tied to productivity or compliance, those beliefs often continue into adulthood.

2. **Societal pressures:** the constant messaging from society about what it means to be successful, happy, or fulfilled can cause you to mold yourself to fit those ideals, rather than honoring your own truth.

3. **Past experiences:** when you have felt validated, loved, or accepted only under certain conditions, it reinforces the belief that your worth is conditional. You begin to live according to what brings approval rather than what feels authentic.

In my story of coming home stressed and snapping at my kids, the gap showed up as the pressure to be a certain kind of parent—one who maintains order and discipline. My upbringing conditioned me to believe that good parenting was about control and productivity. When my daughter confronted me, I realized that what my family truly needed was connection and compassion, not rigid adherence to outdated expectations.

Research by Dr. Leon Festinger in *A Theory of Cognitive Dissonance* shows that cognitive dissonance occurs when there is a conflict between our beliefs and our actions, causing mental discomfort (1957). This discomfort often drives us to change our beliefs, behaviors, or perceptions to create harmony. When my daughter voiced her frustration, it created cognitive dissonance within me. My belief that I was being a good parent by enforcing chores clashed with the reality that my approach was creating disconnection and frustration. This discomfort pushed me to question my own actions and beliefs.

Dr. B.F. Skinner found that habits and behavioral patterns are often reinforced through conditioning, and positive or negative reinforcement shapes how we respond to situations (1938). My automatic reactions to my children were conditioned responses, reinforced over years of believing that discipline and productivity were necessary. When you hold a belief about who you think you should be, your mind creates narratives to support that belief, including thoughts like, *"I have to maintain control to be a good parent,"* or *"If I'm not productive, I'm failing."*

These thoughts reinforce the gap between your true self and the idealized self. Cognitive dissonance occurs when your mind recognizes that your actions are not in alignment with your true desires or values. Awareness of this gap allows you to consciously choose new thoughts that align with your true self. When you are living out of alignment, your body holds tension and stress. Chronic stress from trying to meet unrealistic expectations can manifest as physical symptoms: tension in your shoulders or neck, headaches or fatigue, digestive issues, or general unease.

These physical sensations are often signals from your body, trying to alert you to the disconnection between your actions and your true self. Living from an idealized version of yourself disconnects you from your own truth and intuition. Spiritually, this gap represents a disconnection from your authentic self, your higher purpose and inner wisdom. When you are out of alignment, your spirit feels stifled, suppressed by layers of conditioning and societal expectation. Embracing your true self requires stripping away those layers to connect with your own wisdom and truth.

When you live from a place of who you think you *should* be, your actions are driven by fear, obligation, and external validation. When you live from who you truly are, your actions are guided by love, authenticity, and alignment with your purpose.

Questions for Reflection:

What beliefs are guiding your actions and decisions right now? Are they truly yours or have they been shaped by external expectations?

_____

_____

_____

_____

How does your body respond when you are acting from a place of fear or obligation rather than authenticity?

_____

_____

_____

_____

When you imagine living from your true self, how does your mind, body, and spirit feel different?

_____

_____

_____

_____

Identifying Patterns of Self-Sabotaging Beliefs & Unconscious Habits That Keep You Stuck

Self-sabotage isn't always about dramatic acts of self-destruction. Often, it's the small, unconscious choices and habits that keep you from moving forward. These habits can feel comforting because they are familiar, but they ultimately keep you in a cycle of feeling stuck. Recognizing and shifting these patterns is essential for true transformation.

Common Patterns of Self-Sabotage:

- Procrastination: Delaying action because, deep down, you fear failure or success. By putting things off, you avoid the discomfort of facing potential judgment or disappointment.

- People-Pleasing: Saying yes when you mean no to avoid conflict or rejection. This behavior often stems from a desire to be liked or accepted, even at the expense of your own well-being.

- Negative Self-Talk: Internal dialogues that reinforce a sense of unworthiness, including thoughts like, "I'm not good enough," "I don't deserve success," or "It's safer to stay small than to be seen and judged." These behaviors are often rooted in limiting beliefs that have been reinforced over time. They become unconscious habits that shape your actions, often without you even realizing it.

The pattern of snapping at my kids was a learned response, shaped by how I was raised and what I believed parenting should look like. My upbringing instilled a belief that discipline equaled love and that productivity was the highest measure of success. This unconscious habit of focusing on tasks over connection was a form of self-protection, but it was also a barrier to the closeness I truly wanted with my family.

I was angrier at myself than I was at my children. I realized that the stress from work and my desire to maintain control were sabotaging my family dynamics. Reflecting on this story, I began to see how these patterns weren't just reactions. They were deeply rooted habits shaped by my past experiences and conditioned beliefs. I wasn't intentionally choosing frustration or anger; those were the default settings programmed into me through years of operating on autopilot. And until I became aware of them, they continued to run my life.

Dr. Charles Duhigg, author of *The Power of Habit*, notes that habits are formed through a three-part process: Cue, Routine, and Reward (2012). This "habit loop" becomes embedded in the brain's basal ganglia, making behaviors automatic over time. My automatic reaction of snapping at my kids was a conditioned response based on years of stress, expectation, and the belief that productivity equaled worthiness.

Cue: A trigger that initiates a habitual response. In my story, the cue was coming home to undone chores, which triggered my reaction of frustration. Routine: The habitual response itself. In my case, snapping at my children because I felt overwhelmed by work stress and unfulfilled expectations. Reward: The perceived benefit of the response. The brief feeling of control or release of anger temporarily soothed my underlying frustration.

Just as I had unknowingly reinforced negative habits through repetition, I could also create new, positive habits by consciously choosing different responses. When I decided to respond to my children with curiosity instead of frustration, I began laying down new neural pathways. Over time, these pathways became stronger, making the new response feel more natural.

Cognitive distortions are habitual, inaccurate thinking patterns that often drive self-sabotaging behaviors. They act as mental shortcuts your brain uses to interpret the world, but they can reinforce limiting beliefs and unhelpful habits. Dr. Aaron T. Beck, the founder of cognitive therapy, identified several common distortions that reinforce negative beliefs:

- All-or-Nothing Thinking: Believing that if something isn't perfect, it's a total failure.

- Overgeneralization: Drawing broad conclusions from a single experience, often using words like "always" or "never."

- Catastrophizing: Imagining the worst possible outcome, even if it's unrealistic.

- Mental Filtering: Focusing only on the negative aspects of a situation and ignoring the positives (1979).

My belief that productivity and control were essential for being a good parent was rooted in all-or-nothing thinking. When I wasn't achieving that ideal, I felt like a failure, reinforcing the cycle of frustration and criticism. Recognizing these distortions allowed me to challenge them and begin changing my habitual responses. The patterns I noticed in my reactions to my children were rooted in cognitive distortions. I was operating under the belief that if I didn't maintain control, I was failing as a parent. This all-or-nothing thinking kept me stuck in a cycle of frustration and guilt. When my daughter called me out on my behavior, it forced me to confront these distortions and challenge them.

From a scientific perspective, understanding cognitive distortions provides clarity around why certain behaviors persist. It's not just about breaking habits; it's about examining the underlying thoughts that drive those habits. When I reframed my thoughts and allowed myself to act from a place of compassion rather than fear, I began to shift my patterns. Cognitive distortions shape your perception of yourself and your experiences. When your mind is operating from a place of fear, obligation, or conditioned beliefs, it's difficult to break free from habitual reactions. Becoming aware of these distortions allows you to consciously challenge them and choose new, empowering beliefs. The body often reflects unresolved emotional patterns. Self-sabotaging habits can manifest as tension in the shoulders or jaw, fatigue from constantly striving for perfection, or anxiety when faced with tasks that challenge your limiting beliefs. Your body sends signals when you are out of alignment. By paying attention to these sensations, you can begin to understand which habits are supporting you and which are holding you back.

From a spiritual perspective, self-sabotage can be seen as a disconnection from your higher self. When you are living according to conditioned beliefs rather than your true essence, you feel out of alignment. Reconnecting with your inner wisdom requires compassion and authenticity. It involves recognizing which habits are rooted in fear and choosing to replace them with those rooted in love and truth.

Bringing awareness to these patterns is not about blaming yourself but about loving yourself enough to change them. Once you see the habit, you can choose a new way forward, one aligned with your highest self.

Questions for Reflection:

What habits or behaviors do you notice repeating, even when you know they aren't serving you?

_____

_____

_____

_____

What beliefs are driving these habits? Are they truly yours, or were they conditioned by someone else's expectations?

_____

_____

_____

_____

When you visualize yourself living from a place of alignment and authenticity, what new habits emerge?

_____

_____

_____

_____

The Role of Intuition & Body Wisdom—How Your Body Gives Clues About What's Out of Alignment

Your body often whispers the truth long before your mind understands it. Those subtle sensations, aches, or physical responses are more than just inconveniences; they are messages. Learning to listen to them is a key part of connecting to your intuition and aligning with your true self. I had been ignoring my body's signals for years. The tightness in my chest, the constant

Your body often whispers the truth long before your mind understands it.

headaches, the overwhelming fatigue, these were all symptoms of my body screaming for attention. But I was so busy pushing through, striving to meet everyone else's expectations, that I missed the messages my own body was trying to send me.

When I came home from work stressed out, snapping at my kids was an automatic reaction. The tightness in my chest, the clenching in my gut, or the rush of heat in my face when I was frustrated were my body's way of warning me that something was out of alignment. But instead of listening, I kept pushing forward, reacting from a place of frustration and unmet expectations. I was on autopilot, and my body was trying to wake me up.

Dr. Antonio Damasio, neuroscientist and author of *The Feeling of What Happens*, highlights that interoception is the brain's ability to sense and interpret internal bodily states (1999). Emotions are rooted in the body; they are physical responses that the brain interprets. When you experience discomfort, pain, or tension, your body is providing feedback about your emotional and mental state. Emotions are not just mental experiences; they are deeply physical. This aligns with the idea that your body often reacts before your mind processes what's happening. Becoming aware of these signals can offer profound insights into your emotional state and underlying beliefs.

It wasn't until I began intentionally listening to my body that I could change my reactions. I started noticing the signals before they escalated into harsh words or emotional outbursts. I would feel the tension building in my chest, the clenching of my jaw, or that familiar heat rising when I was frustrated. But instead of snapping, I began asking myself, "What is my body trying to tell me?" That awareness was the turning point. As I began to honor my body's signals and respond with compassion instead of frustration, my relationships improved. I was no longer reacting from a place of old wounds but responding from a place of presence and authenticity.

The mind interprets the signals your body sends, but if you're disconnected from your body's wisdom, you might miss crucial messages. Self-awareness begins with recognizing how your thoughts and emotions influence your body's reactions. Your body is always communicating with you, whether through subtle sensations or more intense physical reactions. Common signals include tightness in the chest, which might indicate anxiety or a need for emotional expression. A clenched jaw can point to repressed anger or unspoken words. Digestive issues may suggest difficulty processing emotions or feeling unsafe. A flushed feeling in the face and neck is often associated with embarrassment, shame, or self-doubt. These sensations aren't random. They're invitations to pause, reflect, and adjust. When I began to listen to my body's messages, I realized that the way I was reacting to my kids wasn't coming from who I truly wanted to be. It was a conditioned response driven by stress, frustration, and unresolved pain.

Spiritually, tuning into your body is about returning to your truth. It's about allowing your higher self to guide you through intuitive insights that arise from the body's signals. When you honor these messages, you align more deeply with your authentic self.

As I learned to listen to my body and follow its guidance, I began to feel more connected to my true self. The frustration and anger that once felt automatic began to dissipate. Instead of reacting from a place of pain, I was responding from a place of love and authenticity. When you learn to trust your body's wisdom, you gain access to a deeper level of guidance. Your body is always working to bring you back to balance and truth. You just need to listen. Have you ever noticed how your body reacts in stressful moments? Take a moment now to check in. What is it telling you?

Questions for Reflection:

What physical sensations arise when you feel out of alignment or triggered? Where in your body do you notice tension or discomfort?

_____

_____

_____

How do your reactions change when you take a moment to listen to your body before responding?

_____

_____

_____

_____

What messages or insights emerge when you honor your body's signals rather than dismissing them?

_____

_____

_____

_____

Action Step: Self-Inventory Reflection Exercise

This exercise is a bridge between awareness and action. It's about pausing, reflecting, and rediscovering who you truly are beneath the layers of conditioning, fear, and expectation. This is your opportunity to find the gaps between your true self and who you're just pretending to be, who you want to be perceived as—to see where you're aligned and where you're not, to acknowledge the patterns that are holding you back, and to begin the process of shifting those patterns with compassion and curiosity. It also allows you to recognize the patterns showing up in your life that are sabotaging you. When you tune into your body's signals and uncover what they're telling you, it helps you open up and become more aware of what you truly want, need, and desire.

The Purpose of This Exercise:

- **Identify Gaps:** Find where the discrepancies lie between your true self and who you feel you "should" be.

- **Recognize Patterns:** Notice which self-sabotaging habits and unconscious beliefs are playing out in your life.

- **Listen to Your Body:** Tune into the subtle signals your body gives you and uncover what they might be telling you.

This is not about fixing yourself. It's about rediscovering yourself. It's about holding yourself with compassion and curiosity as you explore deeper aspects of your being. It's about peeling back those layers and seeing what's underneath, removing the conditioning, removing the fear of judgment. The goal is to create a snapshot of where you are right now with compassion and curiosity.

Reflection Process:

1. **Create Space:** Close your eyes, take a deep breath, and let yourself settle into stillness. Relax your shoulders, unclench your jaw, and feel your body where it meets the surface of your chair or the ground. Allow yourself to become fully present in this moment.

2. **Ask Yourself the Following Questions:**

   o What patterns do I see in my daily reactions and behaviors?

   o Where do I feel most stuck or resistant? What might that resistance be protecting me from?

   o When I'm feeling out of alignment, what do I feel in my body?

   o How different would I feel if I were acting from a place of truth and authenticity rather than fear and expectation?

3. **Journal Your Insights:** As you come out of this reflective space, jot down whatever came up for you. This could be words, images, feelings, or even sensations you notice in your body. Write freely and openly, without censoring yourself.

_____

_____

_____

_____

4. **Return to This Exercise Regularly:** As you continue on your journey, come back to this exercise whenever you feel disconnected or misaligned. Use it as a tool for recalibration and growth.

_____

_____

_____

_____

Summary: Awakening to Your Truth—Understanding Where You Are

This chapter has taken you through a journey of awareness, exploring the patterns, beliefs, and habits that have shaped your experiences. You've begun to uncover the difference between who you truly are and who you think you should be, recognizing the ways in which unconscious conditioning, societal expectations, and past experiences have influenced your reactions and beliefs.

Through my own story of snapping at my children after stressful workdays, you've seen how deeply ingrained habits can become, and how they often emerge from unresolved beliefs rooted in the past. It wasn't until my daughter's honest reflection that I realized the gap between my true self and the parent I wanted to be. This awareness sparked a deeper understanding of how my childhood conditioning and need for control were manifesting in my interactions with my family.

You've also explored the science behind these patterns, including how neuroplasticity allows the brain to rewire itself and form new, healthier neural pathways. This scientific understanding supports the idea that change is not only possible but inevitable when approached with intention and consistency. By consciously choosing different responses and redirecting your focus, you are literally reshaping your brain to align with your true desires.

The RAS plays a powerful role in this process, filtering what you notice based on where your attention is focused. When you begin to shift your focus from negativity to possibility, your brain starts prioritizing experiences that support your growth and healing.

Additionally, you've learned about the connection between your mind, body, and spirit. Your body provides vital signals about what's out of alignment, often manifesting as physical tension, discomfort, or pain. By listening to these signals and honoring your body's wisdom, you can begin to uncover the deeper truths guiding your journey.

Awareness is the first step to transformation. As you continue this journey, remember that self-awareness is not about blame or judgment. It's about compassionately recognizing where you are so you can choose a new path forward. By embracing your truth, acknowledging the patterns that are holding you back, and reconnecting with your authentic self, you are creating the foundation for lasting change.

CHAPTER 3

Living in Purpose: Rediscovering Your Why

Personal Story: Finding Clarity and Purpose Beyond Corporate Success

I remember sitting in a conference room, surrounded by colleagues discussing the latest project milestones. I should have felt proud. I had helped build this company for over 20 years, and it was thriving. But instead, I felt a hollowness inside. Everything I did to build and shape the landscape was only working to fill the owners' pockets. The culture was more toxic than ever. The faces around the table were fixed in fear, sadness, or despair that the next slipup would turn the "guns" on them.

During a brutal verbal assault of one of my colleagues who was holding back tears, I finally spoke up: "This is not okay! You can't treat people this way. We are human beings who care about this company and what we do here. If you want to continue this, I'm leaving this meeting."

Later that day, the owner reprimanded me for speaking up for my colleague and embarrassing the manager who was berating him, who happened to be the owner's son. I knew, after all these years, it appeared the only difference I had made, beyond creating amazing equipment for the research industry, was to help make this man rich, and by being silent for so long, let the toxic culture continue around me. This happened after I returned to work just five weeks after major brain surgery. I was out longer with the natural birth of my children. I was allowing others' expectations to override my integrity, my health, and my overall well-being. I was meant to do more, be more, have a better impact.

I couldn't go back to pretending that success equated to purpose.

Walking out of that meeting, I felt a mix of fear and freedom. I knew I had crossed a line, not just with my boss but with the old version of myself who stayed quiet, who believed her worth was tied to the work she did and the title on her business card. I didn't know what my next step would be, but I knew it had to be different. I couldn't go back to pretending that success equated to purpose. I had a calling beyond this, beyond the corporate ladder.

Leaving the corporate world required a complete shift in mindset. According to Dr. Martin Seligman's PERMA Model of Positive Psychology, true well-being isn't achieved through financial success alone (2011). Instead, it requires a combination of:

- **Positive Emotion:** Cultivating gratitude and joy.
- **Engagement:** Finding flow and full immersion in activities.
- **Relationships:** Deep connections boost well-being.
- **Meaning:** Living with purpose fuels fulfillment.
- **Accomplishment:** Achieving small wins builds momentum.

In my case, corporate success provided accomplishment but lacked the meaning and deep connection I craved. My mindset began to shift as I realized that purpose is about finding fulfillment beyond achievements—about helping others heal and transform. This realization activated a new sense of clarity and determination, opening my mind to what truly mattered. The stress of working in a toxic environment had taken a toll on my body. I could feel it manifesting as tightness in my chest, anxiety, headaches, and constant fatigue. Science shows that chronic stress activates the sympathetic nervous system, our fight-or-flight response, leading to a cascade of physical symptoms. I was stuck in survival mode, with my body bearing the brunt of it.

As I began to align with my purpose, even while still working in that high-pressure environment, I started noticing a physical transformation. My energy levels increased, I experienced less pain, and I felt a renewed sense of vitality. My body was healing as my mind became more aligned. This mirrored findings from **Dan Buettner's Blue Zones study**.

In the Blue Zones, purpose is not just a concept, it's a way of life. In Okinawa, Japan, they call it *ikigai* (EE-kee-guy), or a reason to get up every morning. When I disconnected from my corporate job, I didn't realize I was embarking on my own ikigai journey. But looking back, I see how stepping into my integrity, my authentic self, and my purpose not only transformed my health and happiness but also allowed me to guide others toward their own path of fulfillment. Research shows that this sense of purpose isn't just fulfilling, it's life-extending.

In Buettner's study, they found that having a clear purpose in life can add up to seven years to a person's lifespan! Can you imagine what could happen if you had seven more years? You could see grandchildren grow, attend more family and social functions, and maybe even write a book. It also linked a strong sense of purpose to a 30% reduction in the risk of cardiovascular events, including heart attack and stroke. A clear purpose initiates overall well-being.

The emotional and mental impact is that it contributes to emotional stability and greater life satisfaction and reduces the risk of anxiety and depression by providing a sense of direction and hope. The physical health impact is that we engage in more physical activity, make healthier lifestyle choices, and maintain strong social connections, which are vital for cognitive health and emotional support. These studies suggest that a purpose-driven life can positively affect gene expression related to inflammation and immune function, too.

The **Japanese concept of** *ikigai*, a reason for being, reminds us that purpose often lies at the intersection of what we love, what we're good at, what the world needs, and what we can be rewarded for: our superpowers! When I finally let go of societal expectations and trusted my own intuition, I found myself aligned with my true calling. In spirituality, this process is about coming back to your own truth and embracing your inner wisdom. It's about learning to trust yourself, even when the world tells you otherwise.

Purpose is the bridge between doing and being, between working and living.

Looking back, I realize that corporate success wasn't the wrong path; it was simply a stepping stone. It gave me tools, but it also helped me see the difference between achievement and fulfillment. Finding my purpose was not just about leaving corporate success behind, it was about reclaiming my authentic self. And perhaps, just as I did, you'll find that your purpose is already within you, waiting to be rediscovered.

Now, I guide others not to abandon their paths but to find the purpose woven within them. To live authentically, with intention and joy. Living in your purpose isn't about abandoning what you've built, it's about finding meaning within it. Purpose is the bridge between doing and being, between working and living.

Uncovering and Understanding Your Core Values, Beliefs, Driving Forces, and Energetic Alignment

Core values are the foundational principles that guide your actions, decisions, and interactions. They are the compass that directs you toward alignment and fulfillment. The feelings you feel in your heart and your gut guide you to your truth. In the corporate world, my core value of integrity was constantly being challenged. The culture I was in prioritized profit over people, success over well-being, and productivity over authenticity. It was very much a fear-led culture where decisions were monitored, innovation was stifled, and voices of dissent were quickly silenced.

Every time I watched someone being berated or manipulated, it struck a nerve. It felt wrong, like a betrayal of something deep within me. It wasn't just about the verbal assaults or the unrealistic expectations, it was about the way fear was used as a tool to maintain control.

For years, I stayed quiet, trying to navigate an environment that demanded conformity and compliance. I felt that if I kept my head down and produced results, I could somehow rise above the toxicity. But the truth was, I was only losing myself in the process.

Dr. Martin Seligman's PERMA model emphasizes that meaning and engagement are essential components of our well-being. Living in alignment with your core values directly contributes to a sense of purpose and fulfillment. From a neuroscience perspective, studies show that when our actions are in alignment with our core values, the brain's reward system releases dopamine, enhancing feelings of satisfaction and motivation.

When integrating the mind-body-spirit philosophy, understanding your core values brings clarity to your thoughts. It helps you identify when you are in or out of alignment, providing a roadmap for decisions that honor your true self. When you live out of alignment with your core values, your body feels it. The tension in my shoulders, the headaches, the insomnia—these were all signals my body was sending, begging me to recognize the dissonance. Integrity is a spiritual principle. When I finally honored my own truth, it felt like my soul could breathe again.

Questions for Reflection:

What are your non-negotiable values?

_____

_____

_____

_____

How do you feel physically and emotionally when you live in alignment with them?

_____

_____

_____

_____

What happens when you compromise them?

_____

_____

_____

_____

Our beliefs shape how we perceive the world and ourselves. They can be empowering or limiting. For years, I held onto the belief that success was measured by achievement, status, and recognition. I believed my worth was tied to my work, my title, and my ability to meet impossible expectations. The culture I was in only reinforced these limiting beliefs. The constant monitoring, the expectation to produce more, faster, and with fewer resources, all served to strengthen the belief that my value was based solely on what I could achieve.

The fear-led environment also planted new limiting beliefs: *Speaking up will only lead to punishment. My worth is dependent on my productivity. Success means sacrificing my well-being.*

The story I told myself was that if I didn't excel, I was failing. This belief system kept me pushing harder and harder, even when my health was failing, even when my spirit felt drained. It took me years to understand that this was just a story, a narrative rooted in societal expectations and fear, not my own truth.

Dr. Michael Merzenich's work on neuroplasticity demonstrates that the brain is capable of rewiring itself through intentional effort. When you challenge limiting beliefs and replace them with empowering ones, you are literally creating new neural pathways. When you shift your beliefs, your brain begins filtering information that aligns with your new mindset, making it easier to notice opportunities that support your growth.

When integrating the mind-body-spirit philosophy, beliefs shape your thoughts and actions. Recognizing and challenging limiting beliefs allows for a mindset shift that aligns with your true purpose. Negative beliefs can manifest as physical symptoms like anxiety, headaches, and fatigue. My body was responding to the pressure of trying to live up to unrealistic standards. Spiritual growth requires letting go of old, outdated beliefs. When I began to rewrite my narrative, it was like shedding layers of heaviness and reclaiming my true self.

Questions for Reflection:

What beliefs have been holding you back from living your truth?

_____

_____

_____

_____

How have these beliefs shown up in your mind, body, and spirit?

_____

_____

_____

_____

What new beliefs are you ready to adopt that align with your purpose?

_____

_____

_____

_____

Your driving forces are the passions, desires, and motivations that propel you forward. They are the things that make you feel alive, engaged, and inspired. For me, this was about helping others find healing, clarity, and empowerment. It was about creating a space where people could discover their own truths and embrace their unique journeys, their truths. In the corporate world, I lost touch with these driving forces. I was motivated by external validation rather than internal fulfillment. It was only when I reconnected with what truly inspired me that I began to feel a renewed sense of purpose and energy. I realized that driving forces rooted in fear and obligation will only lead to burnout and disconnection. It was when I began to follow what truly lit me up—coaching, creativity, and spirituality—that my purpose became clear.

Living from your driving forces allows your soul to express itself authentically. It feels like a dance between inspiration and creation.

Dr. Mihaly Csikszentmihalyi's research in flow state and intrinsic motivation shows that when you are fully engaged in activities that inspire you, you enter a state of flow (1990). This state is marked by heightened focus, creativity, and fulfillment. Intrinsic motivation, doing something for the pure joy of it, leads to deeper fulfillment than extrinsic rewards like status or approval.

When integrating the mind-body-spirit philosophy, identifying your driving forces brings focus and motivation. It helps you set goals that feel meaningful and aligned. When you are engaged in work that fuels your passion, you experience increased vitality and well-being. Living from your driving forces allows your soul to express itself authentically. It feels like a dance between inspiration and creation.

Questions for Reflection:

What activities make you feel most alive and engaged?

_____

_____

_____

_____

When do you experience a sense of flow, where time seems to disappear?

_____

_____

_____

_____

How can you incorporate these driving forces into your daily life?

_____

_____

_____

_____

Having energetic alignment is about being in harmony with your true self. It's about feeling connected to your purpose, your values, and your inner guidance. When you are energetically aligned, life feels like it flows effortlessly. When you are out of alignment, everything feels like a struggle. In the corporate world, I was constantly swimming against the current. The more I tried to fit into a mold that wasn't meant for me, the more drained and disconnected I felt. But once I began to honor my truth, everything began to shift. Opportunities aligned, my energy increased, and I felt a deeper sense of fulfillment.

Research by the HeartMath Institute shows that when the heart and brain are in coherence, it creates an optimal state for health and well-being. Coherence is measurable through heart rate variability and is associated with reduced stress, improved cognitive function, emotional resilience, and overall well-being. Achieving coherence between the brain's neural networks enhances clarity, creativity, and decision-making. Research by Dr. Joe Dispenza, who is heavily involved with HeartMath, indicates that achieving coherence between mind, body, and spirit leads to heightened states of awareness, intuitive clarity, and an enhanced ability to manifest desired outcomes (2012).

Alignment begins with clarity. When your mind is focused on your true purpose, it becomes a powerful tool for manifestation. Your body is an energetic vessel. When you are aligned, your physical health flourishes, and you feel a sense of vitality and ease. Spiritually, alignment is about being true to your higher self. It's about listening to your intuition and allowing it to guide you.

Questions for Reflection:

When do you feel most aligned with your true self?

_____

_____

_____

_____

How do you recognize when you are out of alignment?

_____

_____

_____

_____

What practices help you restore energetic harmony?

_____

_____

_____

_____

How Past Experiences, Family Conditioning, and Limiting Beliefs Shape Our Perception of Purpose

Our beliefs often come from a combination of past experiences, family conditioning, societal expectations, and the narratives we build around them. These influences can be both empowering and limiting, depending on how they align with our authentic selves. Growing up, many of us were taught to follow certain scripts: "Climb the corporate ladder." "Security is more important than fulfillment." "Your worth is in what you achieve, not in who you are."

Family conditioning can be a powerful force. We often inherit beliefs about hard work, sacrifice, and conformity. These beliefs may have been passed down through generations, rooted in survival mechanisms or cultural norms—for example, the beliefs that speaking up is disrespectful or that success is only measured by tangible achievements. Limiting Beliefs: "I'm not allowed to want more." "If I walk away from this, I'll be a failure." "I have to sacrifice my happiness for success."

My journey out of the corporate world involved unpacking these old beliefs. I had to shed the notion that success only came in one form and embrace the truth that my path was unique and valuable. The moment I stood up in that meeting wasn't just for my colleague, it was a turning point in reclaiming my voice and stepping into my integrity fully. Recognizing that the beliefs I held were not my own but inherited through conditioning and corporate culture was crucial to my healing process.

Cognitive behavioral therapy, developed by Dr. Aaron Beck and Dr. Albert Ellis, identifies how past experiences and conditioning shape negative thought patterns (1963). These thought patterns often manifest as cognitive distortions, such as black-and-white thinking, catastrophizing, and mind reading. CBT is effective in recognizing, challenging, and reframing these patterns to create healthier beliefs and behaviors.

Dr. Michael Merzenich and Dr. Norman Doidge's research on neuroplasticity demonstrates the brain's capacity to rewire itself. When we challenge limiting beliefs and replace them with empowering ones, we create new neural pathways. This process allows us to break free from past conditioning and form beliefs that are aligned with our true purpose. Neuroplasticity is the brain's ability to reorganize itself by forming new neural connections throughout life. This capacity allows us to change our beliefs, thoughts, and behaviors through intentional effort.

According to the Hebbian Learning Rule, "neurons that fire together, wire together" (Hebb, 1949). This concept explains how repeated thoughts and beliefs become entrenched pathways in the brain, making them feel like truth even when they are merely conditioned responses. By intentionally challenging limiting beliefs and replacing them with empowering ones, you can create new neural pathways. This process requires conscious awareness, repetition, and reinforcement. Reframing negative beliefs into positive ones improves emotional resilience and well-being. According to research by Dr.

Martin Seligman, optimism and positive thinking enhance mental health and cognitive function.

When you identify the patterns that no longer serve you, you can reframe them and create new, empowering beliefs.

When integrating the mind-body-spirit philosophy, understanding your beliefs and conditioning is the first step toward breaking free from them. When you identify the patterns that no longer serve you, you can reframe them and create new, empowering beliefs. Negative beliefs often manifest as physical symptoms, tension, anxiety, and fatigue. Releasing outdated beliefs can lead to physical healing and a renewed sense of vitality. Intuition and inner wisdom are essential tools for identifying limiting beliefs. When you tune into your higher self, you gain clarity about what beliefs align with your true purpose and which ones need to be released.

Questions for Reflection:

What beliefs have you adopted from your family, culture, or past experiences?

_____

_____

_____

_____

Which of these beliefs feels heavy or restrictive, and which feels expansive and empowering?

_____

_____

_____

_____

What intuitive guidance have you received about your true purpose that you may have ignored or dismissed?

_____

_____

_____

_____

How can you begin to release beliefs that no longer serve you and replace them with ones that align with your purpose?

_____

_____

_____

_____

Action Step: Defining Your Purpose Statement

Welcome to this journey of purpose and self-discovery. This is a sacred space to reflect, align, and embrace the deeper calling within you. Whether you arrived here seeking clarity, guidance, or inspiration, know that your journey is unfolding exactly as it should. Purpose is not a title or a job, it's the energy you bring into the world each day. It's how you create meaning for yourself and others. It's the thread that weaves through your experiences, your passions, and the impact you naturally make. We often admire qualities in others because they mirror something inside of us. This action step will help you uncover those reflections and shape them into a personal purpose statement that aligns with who you truly are. Take a moment to ground yourself. Breathe deeply. Trust this process. Your purpose is already within you, this is simply the path to discovering it more clearly.

Step 1: Reflection—Who Speaks to Your Soul?

Purpose often reveals itself through the people we admire. Think about who inspires you, whether they are mentors, historical figures, authors, spiritual guides, or even fictional characters. Who do you feel drawn to and why? The people who inspire us often reflect qualities, values, or strengths we possess or aspire to cultivate within ourselves.

As I began my healing journey, I admired Dr. Deepak Chopra for his ability to blend science and spirituality. His work encouraged me to trust my intuition while also respecting evidence-based practices. I saw myself reflected in his approach to integrative healing.

Make a list of people you admire or who inspire you. Brainstorm as many people as possible without editing your answers or judging who shows up in your mind. They could be family members, mentors, or friends—even authors, leaders, historical figures, fictional characters, superheroes, or spiritual guides. Write down four to eight names that come to mind without overthinking.

- _____

- _____

- _____

- _____

- _____
- _____
- _____

Step 2: Examine Their Essence—Discover the Common Thread

Now, look at the list you just created and sit with it for a moment. Who do you feel a connection to? Did any feel like a kindred spirit or share qualities with your true self? The qualities you admire in others often mirror your own strengths or values waiting to be fully expressed. When you're ready, choose three who resonate most with you at this moment. Write them down below. Don't overthink this.

I realized that the people I admired were all guiding lights in their own way. They inspired transformation, encouraged healing, and empowered others to step into their truth. This insight revealed to me that guiding others was part of my purpose.

Look at the three inspiring people on your list. What are a few archetypes, primary roles, or titles you can give them? This doesn't have to be the name or title that they would call themselves on a business card. This is more about how you see them. Consider what word or words you'd use to introduce each of these people at a dinner party.

Write down the qualities or archetypes these people embody. Are they healers, innovators, creators, teachers, or visionaries?

_____

_____

_____

_____

Step 3: Identify Their Impact—What Is Their Gift to the World?

An archetype's special power is its strength, talent, or winning formula. It's their way of being that makes them stand out to you. What unique qualities have made each of these people so impactful? Don't worry about choosing the "right" special power for each person, just choose the one that resonates with you.

Reflect on the impact or legacy each person has on the world. What do they give? What do they leave behind? What changes do they inspire in others? Purpose is often revealed through the impact you feel called to create. Recognizing the impact of others helps you define the impact you wish to make.

The people I admired helped others find clarity, peace, and healing. They empowered people to transform their lives and connect with their true selves. This made me realize that my purpose was also rooted in empowering others to find their own truth.

What impact do the people you admire have on others? How do they make people feel? What do they inspire or heal?

Step 4: What Resonates With You—Aligning With Your Purpose

Now, turn the qualities and impact you identified outward. Which qualities resonate most with who you are? What feels authentic and aligned to you? Your purpose will feel energizing and aligned, not forced. You will feel a deep sense of resonance and authenticity when you connect with it.

As I sorted through the qualities I admired, I recognized my own gifts of intuition, compassion, and the ability to guide others through transformation. I felt energized by the idea of helping others find clarity and joy, just as I had.

Review your list of qualities and impacts. Which ones feel most authentic to you? Check in with your body. Does it feel light, energized, or expansive when you think about these qualities?

_____

_____

_____

_____

_____

Step 5: Craft Your Purpose Statement—Putting It Into Words

Use this formula to craft your purpose statement:

"I am the [role] who uses [special power] to [create impact]."

Your purpose statement doesn't have to be perfect or final. It is a living statement that can evolve as you do. What matters is that it feels true to you at this moment.

My own purpose statement emerged from my journey of healing and guiding others: "I am the guiding light who uses intuition and compassion to inspire others on their transformational journey to clarity, joy, and fulfillment."

Write your purpose statement using the formula above. Sit with your statement for a few moments, repeating it silently to yourself like a mantra. Then, speak it out loud and feel it in your heart. If it's resonating with you, get ready to act on it! If it's not, feel free to modify and adjust until it feels true and aligned.

I am _____ who uses _____

to _____

_____

_____

Step 6: Integration Plan—Living Your Purpose

Purpose is not just about creating a statement. It is about living it. Take inspired actions that align with your purpose. Your purpose gains power through action. Aligning your daily decisions and actions with your purpose allows it to take root and flourish.

For me, this meant leaving the corporate world to build a business that helps others find their own healing and fulfillment. I began to incorporate my purpose into everything I did, from coaching sessions to workshops and speaking engagements.

How can you incorporate your purpose statement into your daily life? List one action you can take today that aligns with your purpose.

_____

_____

_____

_____

Summary: From Misalignment to Meaning: The Power of Choosing Purpose

You have taken a deep dive into understanding your purpose and how it integrates with your mind, body, and spirit. As you continue this journey, keep returning to the questions that challenge and expand your understanding. Your purpose is not fixed; it is ever-evolving, just as you are.

Every time you realign with your purpose, you strengthen the foundation upon which your mind, body, and spirit can flourish. By living intentionally, you are not only transforming your own life but creating a ripple effect of healing and growth for those you guide and inspire.

Reflecting on that pivotal moment in the conference room, I can now see how deeply misaligned I was with my true purpose. The corporate culture I was immersed in valued profit over people and productivity over authenticity. This clash with my core value of integrity created a disconnect that was not just emotional but physical. My body was responding to the constant stress of an environment that did not honor who I truly was.

Leaving that environment was not just about changing jobs, it was about reclaiming my own truth. It meant confronting limiting beliefs and breaking away from the narratives I had absorbed about success and achievement. As I realigned with my core values, beliefs, and driving forces, I began to experience real clarity and fulfillment.

Mind, body, and spirit are all essential components of purpose. The clarity I gained from reconnecting with what mattered to me most ignited my mental focus. Physically, my body responded by releasing tension and embracing healing. Spiritually, I began to feel aligned and empowered, trusting my intuition to guide me.

The science supports what I experienced. Dr. Martin Seligman's PERMA model highlights the importance of meaning and engagement as foundational elements of well-being. Dan Buettner's Blue Zones study shows that a clear sense of purpose can enhance both longevity and quality of life.

The Japanese concept of *ikigai* demonstrates how fulfillment is found at the intersection of passion, talent, service, and value.

Purpose is not a fixed destination. It evolves as you do. Reconnecting with your purpose is about returning to your core values, listening to your intuition, and aligning your actions with your truth. As you continue this journey, you are building a foundation that allows your mind, body, and spirit to thrive.

But the greatest lesson is that purpose is not something you find, it's something you choose. And when you choose it, your mind, body, and spirit begin to work in harmony, guiding you toward the life you are meant to live.

CHAPTER 4

Vision, Intention & Goals: Creating Your Path Forward

Personal Story: A Time When Setting Clear Intentions Led to Unexpected Breakthroughs

I had intentions of creating a business to help people suffering from mental and emotional issues due to medical trauma and CPTSD. The catalyst for this intention started small, with something that began as a survival tool: bullet journaling. About five months before my brain tumor diagnosis, I started bullet journaling to help me manage the constant flow of symptoms, appointments, and emotions that Lupus brought into my life. It reflected my healing journey in real time. It was a lifeline. I needed something concrete, something that felt like control in a world that felt like it was spinning out of my hands.

At first, bullet journaling was purely functional. Each page was filled with lists of medications, symptoms, pain levels, and doctor visits. But it quickly became so much more. It became a safe space to express gratitude, track my well-being, and find comfort in routines that nurtured my body and mind. This tool helped me to write my gratitude daily, so I would maintain the positive energy my mind and spirit needed to heal my body. It helped track my pain levels so that I could understand what was helping and what was depleting me. It helped keep me on pace with my daily yoga and meditation practice and was a way to use my voice and spill my feelings and experiences onto paper.

I wrote down what I was grateful for every single day, no matter how small or difficult things felt. Gratitude was a powerful practice, a deliberate choice to focus on the positive despite the chaos. The simple act of writing down something I was grateful for each day was transformative. It wasn't just about listing nice things; it was about choosing to see light where there was darkness. I began noticing the subtle moments of joy, moments I might have otherwise overlooked: a good night's sleep, a hug from my children, a moment of calm in a sea of pain. The more I focused on gratitude, the more I felt it expanding within me. That practice alone was helping to rewire my brain to see the positive rather than fixating on the pain and struggle. By intentionally cultivating gratitude, I was building a reserve of positivity to draw from during harder days. The bullet journaling was also a way to organize my life amid the chaos of chronic illness, providing a sense of control and clarity.

But my journaling practice didn't stop there. After the tumor smothering my brain was removed, my creative abilities blossomed like a large peony. I began to explore using drawing, painting, and other forms of media to create pages I loved to look at every day and that brought me joy. That creative expression was healing in itself, a release from the constant focus on symptoms and appointments. Creativity brought me back to myself and reminded me that I was more than just my illness. I even created an Instagram account, @crystal.journals, to share my journal with the world. It was a way of not only processing my experience but also connecting with others who might be struggling. I wanted to create journals that people could use to help heal from the stress of dealing with chronic health conditions, as I had.

In January 2020, a few months before the pandemic, I created a vision board in my journal. That vision board wasn't just a collage of hopes and wishes; it was an intentional tool for visualization. It included images and words that represented everything I wanted to create in my life: healing, joy, creativity, and purpose. It held visions of opening my own business to offer these healing journals, embracing joy through dancing again, paying off our debt, and achieving financial stability so I could leave the toxic corporate life, travel more, and seek adventures, like visiting Hawaii. What started as a

Creativity was more than just an outlet; it was a bridge to healing and purpose.

personal practice became the foundation for my future. I saw how my creativity could help others find clarity and healing, just as it had helped me. My vision board wasn't just a collage of hopes but a living roadmap that guided me toward opportunities and showed me that my pain had a purpose. It was a declaration of what I wanted my life to become. I began to see myself not only as someone recovering but as someone creating a life, a business, and a legacy.

Looking back, I see how every intention I set, every page I filled in my journal, and every vision I placed on my board became a thread in the tapestry of my new life. Creativity was more than just an outlet; it was a bridge to healing and purpose. I see how that simple intention to create a life filled with healing and purpose was the first step toward building the life I live today. It wasn't a straight path, but every twist and turn brought me closer to the vision I had set for myself. All of the things on that vision board came to fruition—many in different ways than I intended, but all towards my greater purpose.

Setting clear intentions was not just about knowing where I wanted to go. It was about creating a vision for a life filled with healing, joy, and purpose. My bullet journal and vision board became tools of transformation, showing me that every step, no matter how small, was part of a larger journey. Through creativity, I not only found my path but also built a bridge to guide others toward their own healing.

Visualization Techniques Backed by Brain Science

Visualization is more than just a creative exercise; it's a scientifically backed tool that can transform your reality. It allows you to create a mental blueprint of your desired future, engaging your brain in ways that align your thoughts, emotions, and actions toward achieving your goals. When you visualize your goals, you are actively engaging the brain's reward system, which boosts motivation and promotes well-being. This is part of what **Dr. Martin Seligman's PERMA** model refers to.

Positive Emotion involves cultivating gratitude and joy to help create a reservoir of resilience. By writing down daily gratitude in my journal, I was actively fostering positive emotions.

Engagement comes from finding flow through creativity and visualization, which helped me achieve peak performance. The more I immersed myself in the act of creating, the more I experienced that sense of timeless focus and engagement.

Relationships were strengthened by sharing my journaling journey through social media, which connected me to others and deepened my sense of purpose.

Meaning emerged as I visualized a life filled with creativity, healing, and purpose, providing me with a powerful sense of meaning and fulfillment.

Accomplishment grew with each journaling entry or drawing I completed, reinforcing a sense of achievement and boosting my self-efficacy.

When I first started bullet journaling, it was simply a way to organize my chaotic life, to track symptoms, and manage the daily onslaught of stress and pain. But as I continued, it evolved into something more powerful. As I added gratitude journaling and creative elements like drawing and painting, I began to see my life differently. I wasn't just tracking my pain and struggle; I was visualizing healing, joy, and creativity. According to Dr. Seligman's research, visualizing positive outcomes helps create new neural pathways, enhancing resilience and overall well-being. When we focus on what we want to achieve, our brain begins to filter information to support that vision. This also ties into the concept of the Reticular Activating System (RAS). Creating vivid mental images of desired outcomes strengthens neural pathways through a process known as neuroplasticity. The more frequently you visualize success and fulfillment, the more your brain begins to believe in the possibility of that reality.

The act of writing down my intentions and creating vision boards wasn't just about wishful thinking. It was a deliberate practice that reshaped how I viewed my future. As I filled my journals with images of healing, creativity, and purpose, my mind began to align with those possibilities. This practice helped me hold onto hope and gave me something to work toward, even when everything felt overwhelming. Solution-focused brief therapy provides further insight into how visualization supports transformation.

One of the core techniques of SFBT is the miracle question, which asks clients to imagine waking up and finding that their problem is completely resolved. By vividly imagining this desired outcome, individuals activate their creativity and resourcefulness, identifying practical steps to move forward. As I visualized myself creating a meaningful business, dancing, traveling, and living a life aligned with purpose, my brain responded. I wasn't just imagining a better life; I was training my mind to recognize opportunities and solutions that aligned with my intentions. This intentional practice built neural pathways that reinforced my belief in what was possible.

Visualization is not about ignoring pain or struggle. It is about creating a mental framework that allows you to transcend it. By intentionally focusing on a desired outcome, you can create new patterns of thought and behavior that align with your vision. This approach blends the science of positive psychology with practical therapeutic techniques, making visualization a powerful tool for transformation.

Visualization engages your mind's creative and analytical abilities. By consciously choosing to focus on positive outcomes, you strengthen neural pathways that support resilience and motivation. Journaling and vision boarding are tools that help you create a mental roadmap for the future you desire. Visualization can influence your physical state. When you imagine yourself achieving a goal or living a joyful, fulfilling life, your body responds by releasing feel-good hormones like dopamine and serotonin. As I created images of healing and joy, I felt my body relax and my pain lessen. Visualization connects you to your higher self, aligning your intentions with your true purpose. It's a way of tuning into your inner guidance, allowing your spirit to guide you toward what feels most authentic and meaningful.

Reflection Questions:

When you visualize your ideal life, what stands out most in your vision?

_____

_____

_____

_____

What feels most aligned with your purpose?

_____

_____

_____

_____

How does your body respond when you imagine yourself living the life you truly desire?

_____

_____

_____

_____

What is one small, tangible action you can take today to bring your vision closer to reality?

_____

_____

_____

_____

Visualization: Seeing Your Future Self

Visualization is about creating a mental picture of the life you want to live and feeling the emotions of that desired future as if it's already real. But it goes deeper than simply imagining an outcome. It's about embodying the energy, emotions, and mindset of your future self.

When I created my vision board, I was doing more than just collecting images. I was intentionally connecting with a future self who was living with purpose, joy, and fulfillment. Those images were visual representations of the energy I wanted to bring into my life. By repeatedly focusing on those visuals, I was training my mind and body to align with that desired future. Through visualization, I didn't just imagine a successful business, I saw myself creating a beautiful product that was deeply meaningful, feeling more freedom, and dancing again. I began to embody the emotions of that vision, feeling the joy, gratitude, and fulfillment as if it were already true. This wasn't just wishful thinking; it was intentional creation.

It's not just WOO!

It's not just WOO! And by "WOO," I mean the limiting belief that anything spiritual, intuitive, or not backed by hard science has no real value. Visualization works because it engages multiple parts of the brain, particularly the RAS. When you visualize something with clarity and emotion, you essentially program your brain to notice opportunities and solutions that align with your vision.

- **RAS in Action:** Studies show that when you focus on a specific goal or intention, your brain becomes primed to notice relevant information and experiences that support that goal. For example, when I visualized building a successful business, I started noticing resources, connections, and opportunities that aligned with that vision.

- **Mental Rehearsal:** Neuroscientific research indicates that mental rehearsal, vividly imagining a desired outcome, can strengthen neural pathways much like actual practice. It's not just about dreaming; it's about training your brain to respond as if the desired outcome is already happening.

- **Positive Psychology & Flow State:** When you engage in creative visualization, you can enter a state of flow, or a heightened state of focus and immersion. Flow states are associated with peak performance and well-being (Csikszentmihalyi, 1990). This creative immersion supports the PERMA model's principles of engagement, meaning, and accomplishment.

- **Quantum Healing Perspective:** From a spiritual standpoint, Deepak Chopra's work on quantum healing highlights that the mind, body, and spirit are interconnected. Visualization, when practiced with intention, can influence not just mental states but also physical health and emotional well-being.

Visualization activates the brain's reward system, boosting motivation and enhancing resilience. By repeatedly focusing on desired outcomes, you reinforce neural pathways that support positive transformation. The emotions you generate through visualization—joy, gratitude, excitement—produce physiological changes. Studies show that visualization can lower stress hormones and enhance immune function. Visualization serves as a bridge between your present self and your higher self. It allows you to connect with your deepest desires and align your actions with your soul's purpose.

Let's take a moment to do a visualization. Close your eyes, take a few intentional breaths, and relax your body into the seat. When you're ready, imagine waking up tomorrow with your life exactly how you've always wanted it to be. Where are you? What are you doing? Who is with you? What emotions are you experiencing? What does your day look like? What do you feel in your body and where? If your future self could give you advice today, what would they say? What is one habit or mindset your future self can embody that you could start practicing now?

Reflection Questions:

When you visualize your future self, what details stand out most?

_____

_____

_____

_____

What emotions arise when you see yourself living your desired life?

_____

_____

_____

_____

How can you bring those emotions into your present reality?

_____

_____

_____

What small, aligned actions can you take today to support the vision you are creating?

_____

_____

_____

_____

The Difference Between Intention & Goals and Why Both Are Needed for Success

Spiritual science insight: Intention is setting an energetic vibration, and goals are the physical actions that resonate with that frequency (*The Biology of Belief*, Lipton, 2005).

An intention is your guiding light. It's rooted in who you are and how you want to feel.

In my journey, I discovered that there's a powerful difference between intention and goals. Understanding this distinction transformed how I approached healing, creativity, and building my business.

Intention is the energetic foundation. It sets the tone and direction for your journey. It's the *why*, the energy, and purpose behind everything else. An intention is your guiding light. It's rooted in who you are and how you want to feel. It's about embodying a mindset that resonates with your highest self. When I first set the intention of creating a life filled with joy and purpose, it wasn't a concrete plan. It was a desire to reconnect with my creativity, rebuild my health, and find meaning beyond the corporate world. That intention gave me direction and clarity. Intentions are about mindset and being. They set a positive tone and keep you aligned with your values and purpose.

A goal, on the other hand, is the tangible step you take to bring your intention into reality. It's the *what* and *how*. A goal is the tangible action that brings your intention into physical reality. It's the *what*, the measurable, actionable steps you take to bring your intentions to life. Goals are specific, quantifiable, and time-bound. They provide the structure that allows your intentions to take form.

My intention was to create a life filled with joy and purpose. My goals were the actions I took to bring that vision into reality. Creating journals, developing a coaching practice, and eventually sharing my story through writing and speaking were all steps toward the life I intended to create. The vision board became a visualization tool that kept me aligned with that purpose. When I looked at it, I could feel the energy of what I was working toward. I could see the life I was building, even if it wasn't here yet. Over time, what started as a simple survival tool grew into something so much more.

Setting intentions wasn't just about having ideas or dreams. It was about creating a roadmap for how I wanted to feel and who I wanted to become. The intention was healing. The goals were specific, actionable steps like developing healing journals, sharing my story, and building a business. This difference between intention and goals is critical. Intention is the foundation, the guiding light. It's the energy and purpose behind everything else. The vision board I created was a tool that blended both. It held the broad intentions of healing, joy, and creativity, but it also contained specific goals like building my business and paying off debt. Every time I looked at that board, I felt the energy of what I was working toward. It was a reminder of my intention and a roadmap for my goals.

Intention Examples:

- "I intend to live a life of peace and purpose."

- "I am committed to prioritizing my well-being by honoring my needs."

- Goal Examples:

- "This month, I will practice daily gratitude journaling and meditate for ten minutes each morning."

- "I will create a daily practice of gratitude journaling to focus on peace and align with my purpose."

Setting an intention is about creating an energetic vibration that aligns with your desired reality. It's like tuning a radio dial to the frequency of what you want to attract. Intention is the energy that flows from your heart and soul. According to Dr. Bruce Lipton's *The Biology of Belief*, our beliefs and intentions can influence our energy fields, which interact with the quantum field to manifest physical results. The energetic resonance of your intentions guides the actions you take, ensuring that your goals are aligned with your deeper purpose. My intention was healing. My goals were the specific, actionable steps I took to bring that vision into reality. It was a commitment. A declaration of who I wanted to become.

In positive psychology, intentions, and goals serve different but complementary purposes. Intentions help cultivate positive emotions and meaning. They create the emotional energy and vision that sustains your motivation. Goals provide the structure for accomplishment and engagement. According to the PERMA model, true well-being is about cultivating positive emotions, finding engagement, building relationships, creating meaning, and achieving accomplishments. Setting intentions helps cultivate positive emotions and create meaning, while setting goals provides structure and momentum toward achievement.

Setting and achieving small, manageable goals builds momentum and reinforces your overall sense of purpose. Studies show that breaking down larger intentions into smaller, achievable goals boosts self-efficacy, the belief in your own ability to succeed. When your intentions are aligned with clear goals, you are more likely to experience fulfillment and resilience, especially during challenges.

According to Dr. Carol Dweck's research on the Growth Mindset, setting goals from a place of curiosity and learning—rather than pressure and perfectionism—allows you to grow and evolve (2006). Progress and fulfillment come from embracing growth and learning. Your intentions are what guide that growth, while your goals help measure progress along the way.

Aligning your goals with your intentions requires clarity. When you know your *why*, your mind becomes focused and clear about the steps you need to take. Visualization and gratitude journaling were tools that helped me keep my mind focused on what truly mattered. Your body responds to both intentions and goals. When you are aligned with your purpose, your body often feels more energized and resilient. When you set goals that are aligned with your deepest desires, your actions feel natural and flow more easily. Spiritually, intentions are the energetic foundation of your actions. Setting an intention aligns you with your higher purpose, which allows you to feel connected and supported by something greater. Goals are the steps you take to bring that higher vision into the world.

My intention of creating a life filled with joy, healing, and purpose wasn't just a wish. It was a commitment—a declaration. And I was actively creating it, piece by piece. When I set the intention, my goals became the practical steps to bring that to life. Creating healing journals, developing my coaching practice, and sharing my story through speaking and writing were all steps toward the life I intended to create.

The vision board became a living tool that helped me balance intention and action. It wasn't just a collage of ideas; it was a practical roadmap that kept me aligned with my purpose. When I looked at it, I could see the life I was building, even if it wasn't fully there yet. That process was about embodying my intentions while actively working toward them. What started as a simple survival tool grew into something so much more. It grew into a method of transformation. The vision board and the journal weren't just tools; they were bridges to a new way of being. And they continue to guide me, reminding me of what truly matters.

Reflection Prompts

What is one intention you want to set for your life right now?

_____

_____

_____

What specific goal could help you live out this intention daily?

_____

_____

_____

_____

How can you ensure your goals are aligned with your deeper purpose?

_____

_____

_____

_____

How Energy, Manifestation, and Aligned Action Create Results

Manifestation isn't just about wishing for something to happen. It's about aligning your thoughts, energy, and actions with your intentions and trusting that the universe will meet you halfway. It's about bringing what you truly desire from thought to reality through conscious, consistent effort. What I've learned along my journey is that manifestation isn't passive. It's not about sitting back and waiting for things to change. It's about creating change by embodying the energy of what you want and then taking real, aligned actions to support it. It's the combination of intention, belief, and action that creates results. What you believe, you can achieve!

When I was recovering from my brain tumor and struggling with Lupus, I had a powerful realization. Every intention I set, every goal I worked toward, was supported by the energy I was putting into it. Whether it was creating healing journals, building a business, or dancing again, none of it happened by accident. It happened because I committed to showing up every day with the energy of healing, creativity, and joy.

It's easy to overlook how much energy matters. We all have an energetic field that interacts with the world around us. According to Deepak Chopra's work on quantum healing, our intentions influence that energy field, affecting how our desires and efforts manifest into physical reality. Essentially, your thoughts, emotions, and beliefs are part of a vibrational frequency that interacts with the universe. When you align your energy with your intentions, you set the stage for transformation.

But here's the key: taking aligned action. Setting intentions is only part of the process. I had to actually do the work. I created vision boards, established daily gratitude practices, and put my creativity into building something meaningful. I wasn't just thinking about change, I was living it. The more I aligned my actions with my intentions, the more opportunities seemed to appear. It felt like the universe was responding to the energy I was putting out. When you combine positive psychology practices like gratitude, visualization, and intentional action, you're literally rewiring your brain to support your desires.

Positive psychology shows us that taking action from a place of joy, gratitude, and intention boosts your motivation and creates a momentum that carries you forward. It's not just about having a positive mindset, it's about actively working toward what you want and trusting the process. I could have easily stayed in the negative victim mentality of my illnesses and my toxic work environment. There was a time when I did. It was so easy to stay there, to let the pain and struggle of my circumstances define me. But I realized the longer I stayed there, the more it affected every other area of my life. It wasn't how I wanted to live. I knew I deserved more. We all do. Shifting my energy was the biggest switch to my healing. It was the choice to focus on what I wanted to create, rather than what was holding me back.

Manifestation is more than just mental work. It involves integrating your mind, body, and spirit to bring your desires into reality. Your thoughts and beliefs shape your reality. Positive psychology emphasizes the importance of focusing on what you want, not just what you fear. When you consistently choose gratitude, joy, and intention, you're aligning your mind with your highest vision.

Your body is your instrument for taking action. Through practices like journaling, creative expression, and physical movement, I grounded my intentions in the physical world. The energy I carried within my body was reflected in the actions I took. Even something as simple as dancing was a way to embody the joy and freedom I was creating. Spiritual alignment means connecting with your higher self, the part of you that understands your true purpose. Intention setting is a spiritual practice. When you align your energy with your intentions, you are tuning into your soul's desires. Trusting the process and allowing your intuition to guide you is just as important as taking action.

Deepak Chopra's research aligns with my own experience. When your mind, body, and spirit are working together, you are far more powerful than when you are operating from only one part of yourself. True manifestation happens when all aspects of your being are in harmony.

Reflection Questions:

What energy do you need to embody to manifest your intention?

_____

_____

_____

_____

What aligned actions can you take today to support your intentions?

_____

_____

_____

_____

How can you bring your mind, body, and spirit into harmony to support your goals?

_____

_____

_____

_____

Action Step: Intention & Goal Setting Exercise

This is your time to take everything you've uncovered in this chapter and put it into practice. Your reflections, visions, and desires are ready to be turned into real, tangible steps. It's about moving from awareness to intention, from intention to action, and from action to manifestation. You've explored your deeper desires, connected with your future self, and uncovered what truly matters to you. Now, it's time to direct your energy toward what you really want, need, and desire.

This process will help you solidify your intentions, define your goals, and take aligned actions that move you closer to your vision. It's not just about setting goals. It's about anchoring your energy into those goals and trusting the process.

1. Set a Clear Intention

Reflect on everything you've discovered in this chapter. What truly matters to you and what is calling you forward? Your intention is your guiding light. It's the energy you want to embody and the essence of what you are working toward. It connects your mind, body, and spirit to your highest vision.

This is the moment to take all that insight and transform it into a powerful, clear intention.

Intention Examples:

- "I intend to live a life filled with creativity and purpose."

- "I am committed to prioritizing my well-being by honoring my needs."

- Take a deep breath. Connect to your breath and the feelings in your body.

What is your most important intention right now?

_____

_____

_____

_____

2. Define a Specific Goal

Now, let's turn that intention into something you can actively work toward. Something concrete and measurable. Goals are the tangible steps that bring your intention to life. They give you a clear roadmap to follow and help you measure your progress. These goals should align with your intention and reflect the energy you want to embody. They are the bridge between your intention and reality. Remember, goals are specific, quantifiable, and time-bound.

Goal Examples:

- "This month, I will create a daily practice of bullet journaling to capture my ideas and intentions."

- "I will meditate for ten minutes each morning to align with peace and clarity."

What goal can you create to support your intention?

_____

_____

_____

_____

3. Identify One Aligned Action

Intentions and goals are powerful, but without aligned action, they remain ideas. Manifestation is about doing the work. Taking real, inspired steps forward. This is where you start to build momentum and direct your energy toward what you truly desire.

Reflect on everything you've uncovered in this chapter. What aligned action can you take right now to support your intention and goal?

Aligned Action Examples:

- "Today, I will spend ten minutes adding to my vision board, focusing on the energy of joy and creation."

- "Today, I will practice gratitude journaling to cultivate positive energy."

What aligned action will you take today?

_____

_____

_____

_____

4. Preparing for Challenges: What Could Go Wrong?

It's easy to get excited about your intention and goals, but life will throw challenges your way. Preparing for potential obstacles will help you remain resilient and stay on course.

Consider:

- What could get in the way of you achieving your goal?

- How might doubt, fear, or old habits try to sabotage your progress?

- What external challenges could arise? (Time constraints, lack of support, etc.)

- Now, brainstorm solutions or adjustments you can make to stay aligned with your intention.

_____

_____

_____

_____

5. Create Your Intention Statement

This step is about turning your intention into a powerful declaration that you can revisit whenever you need clarity or motivation. An intention statement provides direction, affirmation, and energy to your vision.

Intention Statement Example:

- "I am creating a life of joy, purpose, and fulfillment by embracing creativity, healing, and aligned action."

- "I am fully committed to living a balanced, peaceful life rooted in authenticity, compassion, and inner strength."

Write your own intention statement. Make it personal, present-tense, and filled with emotion.

_____

_____

_____

_____

6. Release to the Universe: Let Go of Control

You've done the work to create your vision, set your intentions, and define your actions. Now, it's time to release any attachment to the outcome and trust the process. Manifestation involves both effort and surrender.

Rituals of Release:

- Write your intention on paper and safely burn or shred it as a symbolic act of letting go.

- Practice a gratitude meditation, affirming, "I trust the universe to bring my intention to life in perfect timing."

- Visualize your intention as already complete and feel the joy, peace, or fulfillment that comes with it.

What will your ritual of release be?

_____

_____

_____

_____

The journey you've taken through this chapter has been about more than just setting goals. It's been about connecting deeply with your true self, understanding what you truly desire, and creating a pathway to bring those desires to life.

You deserve to create a life that reflects your highest self. You deserve to feel joy, fulfillment, and alignment. By setting clear intentions, mapping out your goals, and taking aligned actions, you are already stepping into the life you envision. Every small step forward is a victory, bringing you closer to the fulfillment and joy you deserve.

Remember, intentions set the course, goals build the path, and aligned actions bring you closer to your future self. Revisit your intentions and goals regularly. Use this book, a vision board, or a journal as a tool to stay focused and inspired.

Summary: Vision, Intention & Goals—Creating Your Path Forward

This chapter is about more than setting intentions or creating goals. It's about taking everything you have discovered about your true self, your desires, and your vision and turning it into something tangible. Then, aligning your mind, body, and spirit to bring your desires into reality. It's about creating a life that feels meaningful, joyful, and purpose-driven.

When I began bullet journaling, it was a way to cope with the chaos of my symptoms, appointments, and emotions from living with Lupus. It provided clarity and a sense of control when everything felt overwhelming. But what started as a survival tool quickly evolved into something deeper. As I added gratitude journaling and creative expression through drawing and painting, I began to see my life through a different lens. Gratitude became a powerful daily ritual that allowed me to focus on moments of joy. Writing down what I was grateful for wasn't just about listing nice things; it was about deliberately choosing to see light where there was darkness.

You have reflected deeply, visualized your future self, and aligned with your highest purpose. Now, it is time to move from intention to action. This is where your energy and focus begin to shape your reality. Setting clear intentions is about more than just having dreams or wishes. It is about tuning into the energy of what you want and anchoring it through specific, actionable goals. Intention sets the course, and goals build the path. Aligned action is where the magic happens.

During my recovery from the brain tumor, creativity became my lifeline. It helped me reconnect with myself and reminded me I was more than my illness. When I created a vision board in January 2020, it wasn't just a collage of hopes. It was an intentional tool for visualization, filled with images and words representing healing, joy, creativity, and purpose.

That vision board held ideas like opening a business to share my healing journals, embracing dancing again, achieving financial stability, leaving a toxic corporate environment, and traveling to places that inspired me. It served as a guidepost, helping me visualize the life I wanted to build.

As I continued journaling, creating, and working toward my goals, I realized the most powerful change came from shifting my energy. I could have easily stayed stuck in a victim mentality, allowing my illnesses and work environment to define me. There was a time when I did. But the more I stayed there, the more it affected every other area of my life. I knew I deserved more. Shifting my energy was the biggest switch to my healing, choosing to focus on what I wanted to create, rather than what was holding me back.

What I learned was that manifestation isn't just about making wishes or thinking positively. It's about aligning your thoughts, energy, and actions. When your mind, body, and spirit are working together, you are far more powerful than when you operate from only one part of yourself.

However, true manifestation requires a balance between commitment and transformation. At first, I believed my business would be centered around creating healing journals. I poured my energy into that vision, only to realize that my passion for helping others was evolving. As I continued my healing journey, my purpose grew beyond journals. I discovered that guiding others toward healing and transformation in broader, deeper ways was my true calling.

The vision board and journaling were not rigid blueprints but evolving maps that guided me toward my purpose. Staying flexible and open to how my intentions would manifest was crucial. Often, what appears is even greater than what you originally imagined.

Remember, manifestation is a process of integration. Your mind envisions, your body takes action, and your spirit guides you toward your true desires. And through it all, you are not working alone. The universe is supporting you, responding to the energy and effort you put forth.

Pay attention to the signs and synchronicities that begin to appear as you take action toward your vision. Maybe it is a book recommendation that perfectly aligns with what you have been visualizing, or an unexpected connection with someone who can help you achieve your goals. When you are aligned with your intentions, these synchronicities are the universe's way of saying, *"You are on the right path."*

But remember, trusting the universe does not mean forgetting your action plan. Keep moving forward, taking intentional steps, and preparing for potential obstacles. The journey is not always smooth, but each challenge is an opportunity to strengthen your resolve and refine your approach.

Your vision is not just a dream — it is a reality waiting to be created.

This chapter has guided you to create your own roadmap, set intentions, define goals, prepare for challenges, create your intention statement, and release your attachment to the outcome. As you move forward, revisit these exercises regularly. Allow yourself to refine your intentions, celebrate your progress, and realign as needed.

You deserve to create a life that reflects your highest self. By setting clear intentions, mapping out your goals, and taking aligned actions, you are already stepping into the life you envision. Every small step forward is a victory, bringing you closer to the fulfillment and joy you deserve.

Your vision is not just a dream—it is a reality waiting to be created.

The Inner Work: Releasing, Healing & Reframing

CHAPTER 5

Breaking Through Barriers: Understanding Fear & Resistance

Personal Story: A Time When Fear Almost Held Me Back from a Major Breakthrough

A Dual Perspective on Fear

Fear has many faces. It can grip you through your body, hijacking your nervous system and leaving you feeling helpless. It can also creep into your mind and spirit, holding you back from living your truth and embracing who you really are.

I've experienced fear in both of these ways. Sometimes it showed up as physical terror, my body reacting with fight-or-flight responses to the mere sight of a meal. Other times, it appeared as emotional vulnerability, a deep fear of judgment and rejection that kept me hiding parts of myself I wasn't ready to share.

These two experiences of fear, physical and emotional, taught me that true healing requires addressing fear on every level: mind, body, and spirit. Here are two defining moments that taught me just that.

Eating Out After Anaphylactic Reactions

The fear of food was not just about physical safety. It was about the loss of control and the unpredictability of my own body. I sat at the restaurant, my eyes fixed on the plate in front of me. The server had just placed the dish down, and immediately, I noticed something was off. My chest tightened, and I felt the familiar prickle of fear crawl up my neck. I could almost taste the sterile air of the emergency room, hear the beeping of monitors. My mind was already bracing for impact, imagining an anaphylactic reaction before the first bite. My heart pounded so loudly I could barely hear the chatter around me. My hands felt cold and clammy, my vision tunneled, and every part of me screamed to get up and run. I wasn't just afraid of the food. I was afraid of losing control, of my body betraying me in a very public way. Each thought seemed to pour gasoline on the fire of my anxiety, and my body responded with a full-blown fight-or-flight response.

The fear went deeper than the plate in front of me. It was a fear of my own body, of its unpredictability, of the betrayal I had felt before when it turned against me. I had been to the emergency room so many times before, gasping for air, eyes wide with panic as doctors rushed to stabilize me. The memory lived in my muscles, in the way my body tensed at the sight of unfamiliar food. I wasn't just facing a meal, I was facing a history of trauma.

For over a year, I avoided eating out. It was easier to stay home, where I controlled every ingredient, every environment. I became a master of excuses, finding ways to sidestep invitations and avoid the vulnerability of dining in public. My world became smaller, not just physically but emotionally. The fear whispered that safety lived in isolation, but deep down, I knew that was not the freedom I wanted.

I realized that my fear was not just keeping me safe; it was keeping me small. It was keeping me from living a full life. I began to practice grounding techniques, placing my feet firmly on the floor, feeling the support of the earth beneath me. I practiced slow, deliberate breathing, using my exhale to signal safety to my body. The first time I sat at a restaurant again, I brought tools with me: a mantra of "I am safe," a small crystal in my pocket, and the quiet strength of knowing that every step forward was a reclaiming of my life.

I realized that my fear was not just keeping me safe; it was keeping me small.

The first bite was more than just food. It was a declaration of freedom. I could feel the tension unravel; a thread pulled from the tight weave of anxiety I had wrapped around myself. My body, once a source of fear, began to feel like home again. With each meal shared, each outing enjoyed, I built a new story—one where I was not a prisoner of my past, but a creator of my present. This experience taught me that fear is a teacher. It showed me where I needed healing, where I was holding onto old stories of vulnerability and betrayal. By shifting my mindset from "I am not safe" to "I am strong and capable," I began to transform my relationship with fear. It became less of a wall and more of a doorway that led to the freedom and joy I so desperately needed.

Coming Out as a Medium

Fear doesn't just show up when your life is on the line. It also appears when you're standing at the edge of something new and uncertain, especially when that something is your own truth.

I stood in front of my laptop, my finger hovering over the "Post" button. My heart pounded; my breath came in shallow bursts. I was about to share publicly that I am a Medium, a truth I had kept close to my heart for years. My mind raced with questions: *What will people think? Will I be judged? What if this changes everything?* As I stood there, I felt a rush of heat rise from my chest to my cheeks. My body tensed, my mind spun with scenarios of judgment and rejection. I could almost hear the whispers of criticism and see the looks of disbelief. My hands shook, and my voice felt trapped in my throat, as if sharing this truth might unravel me. The fear went deeper than the fear of judgment. It

> *The turning point came when I realized that my fear was not a stop sign — it was a signpost.*

was a fear of exposure, of being seen in a way I never had been before. Sharing my truth as a Medium wasn't just about my work; it was about being vulnerable, opening a door to my soul, and standing fully in who I am. I wasn't just afraid of what others might think. I was afraid of what stepping into the truth might change within me.

For months, I had danced around the truth, hinting at my gifts but never fully owning them. I would write a post and delete it, rehearse a conversation, and stay silent. Each time I pulled back, I felt a part of me shrink. The resistance was strong, whispering that staying hidden was safer, easier. But I knew deep down that hiding my truth was a barrier to living fully. The turning point came when I realized that my fear was not a stop sign—it was a signpost. It was showing me exactly where I needed to step forward. I sat quietly, breathing deeply, and asked for guidance. I felt a gentle nudge, a whisper from my higher self: "Your truth is your gift. Share it." I took a deep breath, and with shaky hands, I pressed "Post."

As soon as I shared my truth, a weight was lifted. The fear that had held me captive turned into a breeze of liberation. I expected backlash, but what I received was connection, messages of support, gratitude, and curiosity. Each time I spoke about my gifts, the fear lost its grip. I began to show up more authentically, not just as a Medium but as my whole self, unfiltered and free.

Once I found the courage to own my gifts as a Medium, it was like a door swung open. Suddenly, I could speak about my experiences with raw honesty, including my struggles with illness, my journey through fear, and the wisdom I had gained along the way. The more I shared, the more my truth became a bridge that connected me with others who needed to hear it.

These two experiences showed me that fear has many faces. Sometimes it is a physical response, a tight chest, a racing heart. Other times, it is an invisible barrier, holding back your voice and hiding your truth. But in both cases, fear wasn't a stop sign, it was an invitation to step into more of who I truly am.

Whether it's the fear of eating something that could harm me or the fear of sharing a part of myself that others might reject, the common thread is the choice to face fear head-on and move forward anyway.

True healing requires acknowledging fear from all angles. It requires integrating the mind, body, and spirit to move through it rather than be paralyzed by it.

Fear is not just something to be overcome. It's a teacher, a guide, and sometimes, a catalyst for transformation.

The Biology of Fear: How Your Brain and Nervous System React to Change

Fear is a natural, protective response designed to keep us safe. But when fear becomes chronic or triggered by emotional threats rather than physical danger, it can limit us in profound ways. Understanding how fear manifests in the body and mind is the first step in reclaiming your power from it.

The amygdala is a small, almond-shaped structure in the brain that acts as a sentinel, constantly scanning for threats. It's responsible for detecting danger and triggering the fight-or-flight response. When the amygdala perceives a threat, whether real or imagined, it sends out distress signals, prompting the release of stress hormones like adrenaline and cortisol. This process prepares the body to act quickly by increasing heart rate, tensing muscles, and sharpening focus.

But the brain doesn't always differentiate between physical and emotional threats. Your amygdala will respond just as strongly to a perceived threat of judgment, rejection, or vulnerability as it would to an actual physical danger. In both experiences, the amygdala responded in very different but equally impactful ways.

> *What these experiences taught me is that the brain and body respond similarly to both physical and emotional threats.*

In the restaurant, the amygdala perceived the uncertainty of the food as a threat, causing physical symptoms like a racing heart, a tight chest, and tunnel vision. My body prepared to flee or fight, even though I was simply sitting at a table. This was my brain's way of trying to protect me from a perceived danger, an allergic reaction that had once been real but was not necessarily present in that moment.

When I was coming out as a Medium, the amygdala responded to the emotional threat of judgment and rejection. The thought of people doubting me or rejecting me triggered the same fight-or-flight response. It wasn't about physical safety but about emotional exposure. My heart raced, my hands trembled, and my breath became shallow, clear signs of my nervous system being activated by perceived emotional danger.

What these experiences taught me is that the brain and body respond similarly to both physical and emotional threats. Whether I was fearing an allergic reaction or the vulnerability of sharing my truth, my nervous system reacted in ways that felt almost identical.

Dr. Stephen Porges's Polyvagal Theory (Porges, 1995) helps explain how the nervous system responds to stress and trauma. According to this theory, the vagus nerve, a critical part of the parasympathetic nervous system, plays a central role in regulating our stress responses, acting as a communication highway between the brain and the body. When the vagus nerve is activated, it promotes calmness and emotional resilience. Practices like deep breathing, meditation, and movement stimulate the vagus nerve, and promoting healing. This is why the tools I used, like grounding techniques, breathing exercises, and holding crystals, were so effective in calming my body during those moments of intense fear. These practices work by engaging the vagus nerve and promoting a sense of calm.

According to heart rate variability studies (Thayer et al., 2012), higher HRV is linked to better emotional control and stress resilience. Lower HRV is associated with anxiety, depression, and a reduced ability to cope with stress. The mind and body are intricately linked. The amygdala's activation and the vagus nerve's response demonstrate how thoughts and beliefs can trigger real, physiological reactions. The fear of eating out activated my body's fight-or-flight response just as much as the fear of publicly owning my truth as a Medium. Even though one was rooted in a physical threat and the other in emotional vulnerability, the biological response was strikingly similar.

This is because the brain doesn't distinguish between physical and emotional threats. The fear response is activated by perception, by the stories we tell ourselves about what might happen. And when those stories are rooted in past trauma, the body responds as if that trauma is happening all over again. But just as the body can be conditioned to react in fear, it can also be guided into states of calm and safety. Breathwork, meditation, and grounding techniques are powerful tools that can help regulate the nervous system and release fear-based patterns.

Studies show that thoughts and beliefs directly affect the nervous system, demonstrating the power of reframing stories to reduce fear responses. These studies explain how the amygdala, the brain's fear center, triggers nervous system responses not only to physical danger but also to emotional triggers. But this is only part of the story. From a spiritual perspective, fear can act as both a barrier and a guide. It shows us where we are not aligned with our highest self. Fear often arises when we are stepping into something new, something that challenges us to grow. As I was coming out as a Medium, the fear I experienced wasn't just about rejection. It was a deeper call to embrace my truth and align with my spiritual path. Fear can also be an invitation to connect more deeply with your spiritual self. It's the voice urging you to rise above limiting beliefs and step into your true purpose. When you quiet the nervous system through practices like breathwork, meditation, or grounding, you create space for your higher self to come forward.

Just as the vagus nerve helps calm the body, connecting with your spirit helps calm the mind. Techniques like meditation, visualization, and energy work are not just calming practices, they are ways of aligning your mind, body, and spirit. When you release fear spiritually, you aren't just calming your nervous system, you are tuning into your higher self and acknowledging your true power. It's about releasing attachment to the outcome and trusting that the universe is guiding you where you need to be.

The mind is a powerful tool in shaping your reality. What you choose to focus on creates neural pathways that either reinforce fear or encourage healing and resilience. Understanding the biology of fear is the first step in rewriting your story.

Reflection Questions:

Think of a time you felt intense fear. What was your body's response?

_____

_____

_____

_____

How does your body react to emotional stress compared to physical stress?

_____

_____

_____

_____

What techniques have you used in the past to calm your mind and body? Did they work? Why or why not?

_____

_____

_____

_____

How can you incorporate breathwork, grounding, or mindfulness practices to shift your nervous system from fear to calm?

_____

_____

_____

_____

How do you want to rewrite the story of your fear response?

_____

_____

_____

_____

The Spiritual Perspective of Resistance: Understanding How Fear is Part of Growth

Resistance is a natural part of growth. It often appears just as we are about to step into something new, something that calls us to be more authentic and aligned with our higher purpose.

From a spiritual perspective, fear isn't just a barrier, but a guide. It shows us where we are holding back, where we feel vulnerable, and where growth is waiting to happen. As Deepak Chopra teaches, fear is often a catalyst for transformation. It arises when we are on the verge of something significant, something that will require us to release the old to make way for the new. This echoes the principles of quantum healing. Our consciousness, intentions, and beliefs shape our reality.

Many spiritual traditions view fear not as an enemy but as a powerful guidepost. When fear arises, it signals that we are approaching an opportunity for growth and healing. It highlights the edges of our comfort zone and points toward where expansion is needed. For me, fear has shown up in many ways. It showed up in the restaurant, not just as a reaction to food but as a deeper struggle with trusting my own body. It showed up when I made the decision to come out as a Medium, triggering doubts and worries about judgment and rejection. But what I've learned is that these fears weren't just roadblocks. They were signs pointing me toward healing and authenticity.

Fear teaches us where we are out of alignment with our true selves. It reveals the parts of us that feel unsafe, unworthy, or unseen. It's not just about overcoming fear but embracing it as part of the journey.

Fear teaches us where we are out of alignment with our true selves.

Resistance often appears when you are about to step into your true purpose. It's that voice that whispers, *"What if I'm not good enough? What if they judge me? What if I fail?"* But what if resistance is actually a sign that you are moving in the right direction? When I felt fear about coming out as a Medium, it wasn't just a fear of judgment, it was a signal that I was being called to live more authentically. Similarly, the resistance I felt in the restaurant was not just about food safety; it was about reclaiming trust in my body and life.

From a spiritual perspective, fear and resistance are doorways. Walking through them doesn't make you a new person; it makes you more of who you truly are. Each fear faced is a step closer to alignment with your higher self. In one of my favorite books, *The Seven Spiritual Laws of Success*, Chopra talks about how fear often arises just before a major transformation. It's a sign that we are breaking free from old patterns and stepping into something greater.

According to Chopra's concept of quantum healing, our consciousness and intentions influence our energy fields. When we align our energy with our highest intentions, fear becomes a tool for growth rather than an obstacle. Chopra's research supports the idea that practices like meditation, mindfulness, and intention-setting can reduce fear and support healing. Through these practices, we connect with our higher selves, creating a bridge between our intentions and their manifestation in reality.

I'm in love with the concept of post-traumatic growth, developed by Dr. Richard Tedeschi and Dr. Lawrence Calhoun (1995). It aligns perfectly with the spiritual perspective of fear as a catalyst for growth. PTG is the positive psychological change that occurs after adversity. Their research identifies five key areas of growth: a greater appreciation for life, stronger personal relationships, new possibilities in life, increased personal strength, and spiritual growth.

When I look at my own experiences, I see how facing fear led to new possibilities, increased strength, and a deepening of my spiritual connection. The fear I faced around eating out wasn't just about physical safety, it was about reclaiming my life and trusting my body again. Coming out as a Medium was not just about revealing a part of myself; it was about integrating that truth into every aspect of my life. Each time I confronted my fears, I grew stronger. Not just mentally and emotionally, but spiritually. I learned that resistance is part of the process and that the fears I faced were guiding me toward my true purpose.

From a spiritual standpoint, resistance isn't something to be eliminated, it's something to be embraced. It's a message from your higher self, pointing you toward the areas of your life that need healing and growth. When you face resistance, ask yourself: *What is this fear trying to teach me?* Instead of seeing it as something to be avoided, view it as a guide.

Deepak Chopra's work emphasizes that transformation requires letting go of attachment to specific outcomes. When I first set the intention of building a business through healing journals, I was focused on that specific goal. But as I evolved, so did my purpose. My business didn't manifest as a journal business; it grew into something deeper and broader. The act of letting go, of releasing control over how things unfold, allowed me to grow in ways I never could have predicted. I wasn't just creating a business. I was creating a life that aligned with my higher self.

Reflection Questions:

When you feel resistance, what is it trying to teach you?

_____

_____

_____

_____

What fears are you currently facing? What do they reveal about your true desires?

_____

_____

_____

_____

How can you embrace resistance as a sign of growth rather than a barrier?

_____

_____

_____

_____

Where in your life are you being called to let go of control and trust the process?

_____

_____

_____

_____

Recognizing the Stories We Tell Ourselves, How They Shape Reality, and How to Reframe Them

The stories we tell ourselves are powerful. They shape our reality, influence our actions, and create the lens through which we view the world. These stories are often built from our experiences, traumas, beliefs, and fears. But they aren't always true. And they aren't always serving us.

For so long, I carried stories that kept me small, hidden, and safe. Stories built on fear, self-doubt, and a desperate need to protect myself from pain. The truth is, those stories were trying to keep me safe, but all they did was keep me stuck. They created walls around me when what I really needed was freedom.

In the restaurant, the story I told myself was simple but powerful: _I am not safe. My body will betray me._ It was a story rooted in trauma, reinforced by each allergic reaction, each emergency room visit. That story held me captive, limiting my ability to enjoy life and connect with others. As a Medium, the story was different but just as imprisoning: _People will judge me. I am_

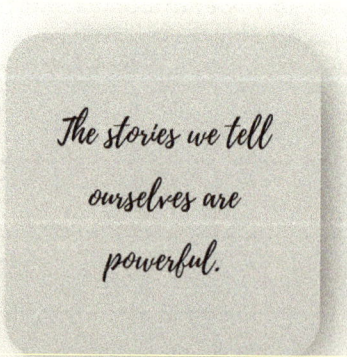

> _The stories we tell ourselves are powerful._

not safe to be seen. It was a story wrapped in fear of rejection and judgment, the same fear that had kept me quiet for years. Sharing my truth as a Medium felt like stepping into a fire. But the only thing burning away was the illusion that hiding would keep me safe.

These beliefs weren't just thoughts, but stories I replayed over and over, training my mind to expect danger, rejection, and failure. And because I believed those stories, my mind and body responded as if they were true.

Our brains are designed to respond to the stories we tell ourselves. When we repeat a belief long enough, it becomes hardwired into our brains. It's like building a road that becomes smoother and easier to travel the more you use it. But just because a road is well-worn doesn't mean it's leading you anywhere you want to go. According to research by Dr. Michael Merzenich and Dr. Norman Doidge, the brain has the ability to reorganize itself based on repeated thought patterns and behaviors. This process, known as neuroplasticity, means that the stories we tell ourselves can physically reshape the brain's neural pathways. Negative, fear-based thoughts strengthen those pathways, making them more automatic and harder to change.

The good news is that just as the brain wires itself based on negative beliefs, it can also rewire itself to support positive, empowering beliefs. When you actively choose new thoughts and beliefs, you are training your brain to adopt a new reality.

The RAS acts as a filter, determining what information is important and worth noticing. When you focus on limiting beliefs, your brain filters your experiences to support those beliefs. By shifting your attention to new, empowering stories, you can retrain the RAS to notice opportunities, solutions, and signs of growth.

The stories we tell ourselves aren't just thoughts floating in our minds. They are deeply interconnected with our bodies and spirits. Thoughts create reality. Science confirms that mindset shifts create real neurological changes. When we reframe limiting beliefs, we are creating new neural pathways that support growth, resilience, and well-being. When I told myself I wasn't safe, my body responded with symptoms of anxiety—a tight chest, a racing heart, and cold sweat. It was the brain's way of protecting me from perceived threats, even when those threats were emotional rather than physical.

Trauma expert Dr. Bessel van der Kolk explains in *The Body Keeps the Score* that trauma is stored in the body and can manifest physically through symptoms and tension (2014). Reframing beliefs through practices like breathwork, meditation, and grounding exercises can help release that stored energy. From a spiritual perspective, the stories we tell ourselves can either align us with our higher purpose or pull us away from it. As Deepak Chopra teaches, fear often signals transformation. When you shift your internal narrative from "I am not safe" to "I am supported and free to be my authentic self," you are aligning your energy with your higher self. It's about tuning into your soul's desires and allowing those truths to guide your actions. The process of reframing is more than just changing thoughts, it's about integrating your mind, body, and spirit to create a new story that aligns with your true self.

The truth is, those stories were never the full picture. They were fragments of pain, fear, and survival. But they weren't my whole truth. Reframing my beliefs wasn't about ignoring my experiences or pretending fear didn't exist. It was about choosing to tell a new story, one rooted in strength, growth, and possibility.

Limiting Beliefs → Empowering Beliefs:
"I am not safe." → *"I am strong, capable, and supported."*
"I am not safe to be seen." → *"My gifts are valuable, and I am safe to share my truth."*

Reframing the stories I told myself required awareness, intention, and consistency. It wasn't a one-time event. It was a daily practice of noticing the old stories, acknowledging them with compassion, and choosing to tell a new one. It was rewriting the narrative of my life, one thought at a time.

It was rewriting the narrative of my life, one thought at a time.

Reflection Questions:

What is a limiting belief or story that you keep telling yourself?

_____

_____

_____

_____

How has this belief impacted your thoughts, emotions, and physical experiences? Notice how your body responds when you focus on this belief.

_____

_____

_____

_____

Where do you feel resistance in your mind, body, or spirit when you hold onto this belief?

_____

_____

_____

_____

Why We Resist Change (and How to Move Through Fear)

Resistance isn't a sign that you're doing something wrong; it's a sign that something is changing. When you're stepping into something new or shedding an old pattern, it's natural for your mind and body to resist. That's because the brain is designed to seek safety and predictability. When it senses something unfamiliar, it often responds with fear, doubt, or procrastination.

This isn't weakness; it's biology.

Your brain's primary job is to keep you safe. It does this by scanning for potential threats, both physical and emotional. The amygdala, the brain's fear center, detects change as a possible danger, triggering the fight-or-flight response. But the brain doesn't always distinguish between real threats and perceived ones. It reacts just as strongly to the fear of judgment or failure as it does to physical danger.

The RAS plays a crucial role here. This bundle of nerves at the base of your brainstem acts as a filter, determining what information gets through to your conscious mind. It highlights what you deem important, which is why when you set an intention or focus on a particular outcome, you begin to notice opportunities that align with your goals. However, when your mind is filled with limiting beliefs and negative thought patterns, the RAS continues to filter the world through that lens, reinforcing resistance. It keeps you stuck in your comfort zone because that's where it believes you're safe.

Research insights on the RAS by Dr. Shad Helmstetter notes that the RAS acts as the brain's filter, highlighting information that aligns with your beliefs, intentions, and areas of focus (1980). Studies on priming (Bargh et al., 1996) demonstrate how what you focus on influences what you notice. When participants were prompted to look for yellow cars, they suddenly noticed them everywhere. This shows how the RAS aligns perception with intention. By setting clear intentions and visualizing success, you can train the RAS to notice opportunities rather than obstacles.

Your mind, body, and spirit are intertwined when it comes to moving through resistance. When you focus on growth, possibility, and healing, your RAS begins to prioritize those experiences. Affirmations, visualization, and gratitude are tools that can shift your mental focus and guide your brain toward what you desire. Fear often manifests physically—tightness in the chest, shallow breathing, racing heart. Practices like grounding techniques, deep breathing, and movement help activate your parasympathetic nervous system, moving you from a state of *fight-or-flight* to *rest-and-digest.*

Spiritually, resistance can be a powerful teacher. It reveals where you are holding onto limiting beliefs or outdated patterns. When you feel that internal pushback, it's often a sign that you're on the verge of transformation. Meditation, prayer, and intention setting can help you connect with your higher self, finding guidance and strength to move forward.

When fear arises, bring your awareness to your body. Feel your feet on the ground, your breath moving in and out. This simple act helps calm the nervous system and reminds your mind that you are safe. Observe your thoughts without attachment. Let fear move through you instead of taking root. Journaling, meditation, and breathwork are powerful tools for shifting your mental state. Call on your higher self for guidance. When you feel resistance, ask, "What is this trying to teach me?" Often, resistance is a doorway, inviting you to step into more of who you truly are.

Resistance is not a wall, it's a threshold. When you move through it, you find not only freedom but a deeper connection to your purpose.

Reflection Questions:

What fear or resistance keeps resurfacing when you consider making a change in your life?

_____

_____

_____

_____

How does your body react when you feel resistance? What physical sensations arise?

_____

_____

_____

_____

What spiritual guidance or insight could help you move through this resistance?

_____

_____

_____

_____

Action Step: From Limiting Beliefs to Empowering Truths

You've explored how fear shows up in your life and how resistance is a natural part of growth. Now, it's time to transform that fear into fuel. This exercise will guide you through identifying the limiting beliefs that are holding you back and rewriting them into empowering truths that align with your highest self.

This is a process of awareness, release, and transformation. When you take the time to do this work, you are actively reprogramming your mind and shifting your energy toward what you truly desire.

Step 1: Identify a Challenging Situation

Think of a specific situation where fear or resistance is holding you back. Write it down objectively, focusing on what happened rather than how it felt. This helps you view the experience from a neutral, grounded perspective.

Example: "I feel anxious about speaking up in meetings at work."

Now, write your own challenging situation:

_____

_____

_____

_____

Step 2: Recognize the Limiting Belief

Ask yourself: "What is the story I am telling myself about this situation?"

The mind creates stories to make sense of the world, but not all of them serve you. Identifying the limiting belief behind the fear is the first step toward rewriting it.

Example: "I am not smart enough. My ideas are not valuable."

Now, write down the limiting belief you've uncovered:

_____

_____

_____

_____

Step 3: Evaluate the Costs and Benefits

This is where you really get honest with yourself. Holding onto limiting beliefs often feels safe because it's familiar but also holding you back.

Costs: What does holding onto this belief cost you in terms of peace, freedom, or opportunity?

Example: "It costs me confidence. It keeps me small and prevents me from contributing my ideas."

Benefits: What do you gain from holding onto this belief?

Example: "I feel safe by not risking rejection. I avoid discomfort."

Now, write down the costs and benefits of holding onto your belief:

_____

_____

_____

_____

Reflect: Is this story worth holding on to?

_____

_____

_____

_____

Step 4: Reframe the Limiting Belief

Now that you've identified the belief and examined its impact, it's time to reframe it. This is about choosing a new belief that feels more expansive and empowering.

Brainstorm alternative beliefs that resonate deeply with your higher self. Choose one that feels true and powerful.

Example: "I am smart and capable. My ideas are valuable and worth sharing."

Now, write down your new empowering belief:

_____

_____

_____

_____

Step 5: Create a New Story

Writing down your new belief is powerful, but it becomes even stronger when you visualize yourself living from this truth. Picture yourself embodying this new belief with confidence and ease.

Affirmations to support your new belief:

- "I trust my voice and share my ideas with confidence."

- "I am safe to be seen and heard."

Visualize yourself stepping into this new story. Feel it in your body, see it in your mind, and allow your spirit to embrace it.

Now, write down your new story:

_____

_____

_____

_____

Step 6: Implement a Daily Practice

Transformation happens through consistent, intentional practice. To fully integrate your new belief, make it a part of your daily life.

- Morning Ritual: Say your new belief aloud each morning. Feel its truth and power.

- Journaling: Write about your new belief and how it feels to live from this place.

The Spiritual Layer: Releasing Limiting Beliefs to the Universe

This step is about energetically releasing what no longer serves you and making space for what truly aligns with your highest self.

Say: "I release the old belief with love and gratitude. I welcome the new truth into my life with open arms."

Visualize your old story dissolving, replaced by the light and clarity of your new belief. Imagine capturing these beliefs in a balloon or bubble and releasing them into the universe. Allow yourself to feel the peace and freedom that comes with letting go.

Summary: Breaking Through Barriers — Understanding Fear & Resistance

Fear has a way of showing up in every corner of your life, whether it's through your body, mind, or spirit. What I've come to understand is that fear is layered; it's not just a physical reaction, it's also emotional and deeply spiritual. Facing these layers is where true healing begins.

My experiences with fear showed up in two powerful ways: the fear of eating out after multiple anaphylactic reactions and the fear of coming out as a Medium. Both of these moments were drenched in anxiety, but their roots were different. One was about physical safety and the unpredictability of my own body. The other was about vulnerability, judgment, and being seen for who I truly am.

These experiences taught me that fear isn't just about danger. It's about control, trust, and being willing to stand in your truth even when it feels terrifying. My body's reaction to fear in the restaurant was real. But what made it even harder was the story I was telling myself: "I am not safe. My body will betray me." Coming out as a Medium was a different kind of fear, but just as consuming. It was rooted in the belief that I wouldn't be accepted for who I truly am. I kept dancing around the truth, hiding behind words that felt safer but were never fully me. Every time I pulled back, I felt smaller, as if I was erasing parts of myself to keep others comfortable.

It took me a long time to see that both of these fears were teachers. They were pointing me toward areas of my life that needed healing. My body's reactions were trying to protect me, but I realized they were keeping me small. And the emotional resistance? That was my higher self trying to guide me toward deeper authenticity.

What I've learned is that the real work isn't about getting rid of fear. It's about transforming it.

Science supports what I've experienced firsthand. The amygdala reacts to both physical and emotional threats as if they are the same. When the amygdala perceives danger, whether it's an allergic reaction or the fear of judgment, it activates the same fight-or-flight response. But understanding how my body works was only part of the journey. Healing required integrating my mind, body, and spirit.

Deepak Chopra's teachings on fear being a catalyst for growth rang true for me. Every time I've faced fear head-on, whether it was eating out or owning my truth as a Medium, it led me to a deeper level of healing and authenticity. It was like breaking through a barrier and stepping into a version of myself that felt truer and more aligned.

Fear doesn't just go away. It's something you have to work with, understand, and sometimes even befriend. What I've learned is that the real work isn't about getting rid of fear. It's about transforming it. It's about noticing when it shows up, understanding why, and then choosing to step forward anyway. Both experiences were about releasing old stories and choosing new ones. And that's where real transformation happens.

Fear is a teacher, not a wall. It shows you where healing is needed and where you're being called to grow. When I look back now, I can see that every time I faced my fear, it brought me closer to who I truly am. And that's a journey worth taking.

CHAPTER 6

Shadow Work & Self-Discovery: Embracing All of You

Personal Story: A Moment When Embracing a "Shadow" Part of Myself Changed My Life

After going through the immense healing in my life, especially dealing with chronic illness, I found myself in a confused state. I had gained all this health knowledge, specifically nutrition from a holistic and healing point of view. There was a time when I would look at others and feel a burning judgment rise up within me. It wasn't just annoyance or frustration. It was deeper, sharper, like a thorn that couldn't be removed. It showed up most fiercely when I saw people neglecting their health, refusing to take care of themselves. I was passionate about healing, about helping others reclaim their well-being, but this passion carried a shadow. It was judgment disguised as care.

I couldn't understand why seeing someone drink soda or make unhealthy choices filled me with such frustration. I would shake my head internally, caught between wanting to help and feeling a disdain that I knew wasn't healthy or compassionate. I was so focused on other people's behaviors that I didn't realize the real struggle was within me.

The truth is, my frustration had nothing to do with them and everything to do with me. It was my own fear and pain being projected outward. I had been battling health challenges for so long—autoimmune conditions, allergies, Lupus, the trauma of repeated anaphylactic shocks—and watching others disregard their health was like watching them risk the very thing I had fought so hard to reclaim. I projected my own pain and fear onto them.

> *What I judged in others was a reflection of the parts of myself I hadn't yet made peace with.*

When I started to do the deeper work of examining these feelings, I realized that the judgment I was projecting was rooted in my own wounds. I was holding on to anger, resentment, and a deep sadness about the times I felt my body had betrayed me. The truth was, I was still struggling to trust my own body and my own healing process fully. What I judged in others was a reflection of the parts of myself I hadn't yet made peace with.

Shadow work became a turning point for me. It allowed me to look at my own judgments and recognize them as unhealed parts of myself. I realized that I wasn't truly angry at those who weren't taking care of their health. I was angry at myself for not having the power to prevent my own suffering. I was angry at myself for not having the knowledge I needed to be healthy in mind, body, and spirit.

Embracing that truth was both painful and freeing. It required me to face the parts of myself I had been rejecting: the fear, the resentment, the sense of helplessness. But once I acknowledged them, I could begin to heal them. I could offer myself the same compassion I was so willing to offer others. And in doing so, I found a deeper level of healing than I ever could have imagined.

This shift in my inner self changed everything. Once I recognized that my judgments were rooted in my own unhealed pain, I could finally let them go. It was as if I had been carrying around heavy armor, convinced it was protecting me, only to realize it was just weighing me down. The release wasn't instant. It was a process of acknowledging, forgiving, and integrating the parts of myself I had kept hidden, including the pain, the anger, and the fear. Shadow work wasn't just about acknowledging my wounds; it was about offering them compassion and understanding. It was about healing the parts of myself I had been pushing away for so long.

Understanding my own shadows allowed me to hold space for theirs.

As I did this work, I began to see others through a different lens. The judgments I once held toward others dissolved into curiosity and compassion. I could see their struggles without projecting my own pain onto them. I could recognize their shadows as reflections of their own unhealed parts, not as flaws or failures. This transformation wasn't just personal. It impacted how I approached my work with clients in a profound way. I no longer looked at their choices through a lens of frustration or judgment. Instead, I saw them as whole, complex beings navigating their own journeys. Journeys that were often filled with pain, fear, and self-doubt, just like mine had been.

Understanding my own shadows allowed me to hold space for theirs. I became more attuned to the subtleties of their experiences, recognizing that their struggles were often rooted in deeper wounds. I stopped trying to force healing through rigid guidelines, expectations, or my own experiences.

Instead, I created an environment of acceptance, where they could explore their own shadows without fear of judgment. But there was another layer of insight that came from this process—a deeper understanding of health itself. I began to realize that true wellness is not just about the individual; it's about the entire landscape of their life. It's not just about the choices people make, but about the environments they find themselves in.

I saw how my clients' struggles with health weren't just about discipline or motivation. They were navigating systems designed to work against them. Bad food choices are front and center at the grocery stores, packaged in bright colors and sold at lower prices than fresh, nutritious options. These aren't just individual choices—they're societal patterns that have become ingrained in how we live.

And it goes even deeper than that. I started to see how upbringing, traditions, cultural expectations, and limiting beliefs all play a role in shaping a person's health journey. People carry the beliefs of their families and communities, the habits formed from childhood, and the narratives that have been handed down through generations. Wellness isn't just about what we eat or how we move; it's about the stories we've been told and the systems we are surrounded by. It's about understanding that the root of someone's struggle might not be their lack of willpower, but rather the limitations placed on them by their environment, their upbringing, or even the subconscious beliefs they've never questioned.

This perspective shifted how I worked with clients. I began to explore not just their habits, but their environments, their histories, and their beliefs. I started asking different questions and diving into the roots of their struggles instead of just focusing on the symptoms. I realized that true healing requires addressing all of it—the physical, the mental, the emotional, the spiritual, and even the environmental. Once I was able to see the whole picture, I could offer guidance that resonated on a deeper level.

This new perspective made me a better coach, a better healer, and a more compassionate human being. It taught me that health is not a single destination to be reached but a journey that encompasses every aspect of a person's life. When we honor all of those aspects, true transformation becomes possible.

The Psychology of the Unconscious Mind—Why We Reject Parts of Ourselves

For a long time, I couldn't understand why I was so triggered by other people's health choices. Why did it bother me when someone drank soda or didn't seem to care about the ingredients in their food? The truth is, those reactions weren't really about them. They were mirrors, reflecting back parts of myself that I hadn't fully acknowledged or accepted. That's the power of the unconscious mind. It stores our hidden fears, unhealed wounds, and protective beliefs, often without us even realizing it.

Psychologist Carl Jung (1959) referred to these repressed parts as the shadow. And when we don't make space to explore them, they show up in other ways, like through projection, judgment, and emotional triggers. What I was really judging in others was the part of me that still felt betrayed by my own body, the part of me that was angry I had to learn the hard way how deeply food and stress could affect my health. Stress had ruled my life for years due to high-pressure roles, health scares, food reactions, and the weight of trying to do it all. My body had been shouting at me for a long time, but I didn't know how to listen. The chronic stress I was carrying wasn't just emotional, it was biological.

According to Dr. Robert Sapolsky, chronic stress keeps cortisol levels elevated over time, which creates a cascade of damage in the body, weakening the immune system, contributing to inflammation, and leading to cognitive decline and autoimmune issues (2004). Dr. Bruce McEwen's research shows that this allostatic load, your body's cumulative stress burden, can literally change the structure of your brain—especially the hippocampus, which impacts memory, learning, and emotional regulation (1993). And isn't that what was happening to me? I was reacting not from logic or compassion, but from a dysregulated nervous system and the wounds still living in my unconscious mind. The judgment wasn't who I was. It was a symptom of my own stress, pain, and unprocessed emotions.

The good news is that the unconscious mind can be accessed and healed. We can rewire these patterns. But it takes more than a shift in mindset. It takes the mind, body, and spirit working together. Becoming aware of the story you're telling yourself is the first step. What belief or fear is underneath your reaction? When I retraced my judgment, it was a deep fear of suffering. I didn't want others to suffer like I did. But fear is not a solid foundation for healing, it must be transformed.

Chronic stress lives in the body. Breathwork, movement, and grounding help regulate the nervous system and reduce cortisol. These tools literally helped me return to safety in my body so I could process emotions instead of projecting them. Shadow work is deeply spiritual. It's about honoring every part of you, even the parts that feel messy or uncomfortable. When I finally made peace with the shadow part of me that had been judging others, I found a deeper connection to my compassion, my purpose, and my truth. It wasn't about being perfect, it was about being fully myself without the fear barrier.

Reflection Questions:

When you feel judgment rise within you, what might it be reflecting back to you about your own unhealed wounds?

_____

_____

_____

_____

How does stress show up in your body? What helps you shift from reaction to regulation?

_____

_____

_____

_____

What hidden or rejected part of yourself is ready to be seen with compassion instead of shame?

_____

_____

_____

_____

What Is Shadow Work and Why Does It Matter?

Shadow work is the process of exploring the hidden parts of ourselves, such as the traits, emotions, and behaviors we've pushed away, judged, or denied. These are often aspects we've been conditioned to believe are "bad," "too much," or "not enough." But the truth is, these shadow parts hold wisdom. They are not meant to be rejected. They are meant to be seen, accepted, and integrated because healing is not about perfection. It is about wholeness. It's about accepting your true, whole self and integrating what you've learned with how you want to move forward with your life.

Carl Jung, the father of analytical psychology, coined the term "the shadow" to describe the unconscious parts of ourselves we disown. He believed that to become truly whole, we must integrate these shadow elements, not bury them. Jung wrote, "One does not become enlightened by imagining figures of light, but by making the darkness conscious." For me, shadow work became real when I realized that my judgment of others' health choices wasn't about them. It was about me. My resentment toward people who drank soda or ignored their well-being was a

> *Shadow work is the process of exploring the hidden parts of ourselves, such as the traits, emotions, and behaviors we've pushed away, judged, or denied.*

reflection of the pain I had not yet healed. I had fought so hard to reclaim my health that watching others dismiss theirs felt unbearable. I wasn't really judging them. I was carrying grief, frustration, and fear about what I had lost and what I couldn't control. Shadow work helped me bring those feelings into the light. It helped me learn so much more about myself, my thoughts, and my emotions.

Doing this work wasn't easy. It required deep honesty and compassion. I had to ask, "Why does this bother me so much?" and "What part of me feels threatened or unseen here?" And when I got quiet enough to listen, I realized it was the part of me that still mourned my own suffering. The part of me that was scared of losing more. The part of me that still felt betrayed by my body. Once I saw that clearly, the judgment began to soften, and compassion took its place.

Shadow work matters because, without it, we are constantly reacting to life from our unhealed wounds. We project our inner pain onto others, we stay stuck in limiting patterns, and we miss the opportunity to show up as our authentic selves. But when we acknowledge and integrate our shadows, we expand our capacity for self-acceptance, connection, and joy. The mind-body-spirit connection is deeply present in this work. The body often stores the emotions we're not ready to feel. That tightness in your chest when you're triggered, or that tension in your jaw when someone says something that hits a nerve, is the body's way of saying, "There's a shadow here waiting to be seen." I like to call this reactionary self the Windsock Guy. You probably know what I'm talking about—the inflatable tube with a head and arms flailing all over at car dealerships and other retail stores to get your attention, like, "Hey, look at me!" When I feel like the Windsock Guy, I ask myself: *Why are you reacting? What is this triggering in me? What is this shadow?*

Spiritually, shadow work is about coming home to your full self, meaning not just the parts you love, but the parts you've avoided. When you meet those places with compassion instead of judgment, something shifts. You start to trust yourself more. You stop hiding. You show up with a depth and presence that only comes from true integration.

This work isn't about becoming someone new. It's about remembering who you are beneath the stories, shame, and conditioning. Your light is only as powerful as your willingness to face your shadow.

Reflection Questions:

What parts of yourself have you judged or rejected that may be asking for compassion?

_____

_____

_____

_____

_____

How do you see your own unhealed pain reflected in the way you view others?

_____

_____

_____

_____

_____

What would it feel like to offer unconditional acceptance to all parts of yourself, even the ones you've hidden?

_____

_____

_____

_____

_____

How to Integrate Your Light and Shadow for True Healing Through Self-Acceptance and Integration

True healing is not about getting rid of the parts of ourselves we don't like. It's about weaving them back into the whole with love. Integration is the process of bringing your light and shadow together so that you can live fully, not fractured or compartmentalized, but as your complete, authentic self. There is a quiet strength in self-acceptance. When I finally started embracing the parts of me I used to push away—the fear, the resentment, the judgments—I felt something shift. Not just emotionally, but physically. My chest softened. My breath deepened. My nervous system stopped firing in all directions, and I could feel my body beginning to trust me again. This wasn't a mindset shift. It was a full-body shift. My heart was guiding the way.

Science confirms this connection. The HeartMath Institute has shown that the heart actually sends more signals to the brain than the brain sends to the heart. That means our intuition, emotions, and inner state are powerful drivers of

There is a quiet strength in self-acceptance.

thought. When we tune into our heart's intelligence, we can change how our brain functions. That is how integration begins, not just in our thoughts but in our physiology. Heart-brain coherence is the state where our heart rhythms and brain waves sync up. It creates a sense of inner harmony where we are more emotionally resilient, more grounded, and better able to make choices that reflect our true selves. When we are caught in fear, shame, or judgment, our heart rhythm becomes chaotic. But when we practice gratitude, compassion, and intentional breathing, our heart rhythm becomes steady. This physiological shift supports emotional healing.

That is exactly what happened for me. As I began integrating the shadows I once rejected, my emotional landscape changed. I became less reactive and more reflective. I stopped seeing my emotions as problems and started seeing them as messages. The parts of me I used to silence began to speak clearly, and I listened, not with my mind, but with my heart. I became my true kinder self.

Integration is not about fixing anything. It invites you to soften. To make room. To hold space for all that you are. The brilliant, the messy, and everything in between. Integration is about deepening into self-awareness while also anchoring into the wisdom of your body and your spirit. Your heart is a powerful guide in this process. According to HRV biofeedback studies, when we practice heart-centered gratitude and intentional breathing, we increase heart rate variability, a key marker of emotional resilience. This is not just about calming down. It is about rewiring your system to support healing and truly coming back to you.

Here is a simple way to begin:

Heart Coherence Integration Practice

- Sit quietly and place your hand over your heart.

- Begin to breathe slowly and deeply. Inhale for a count of five. Exhale for a count of five.

- Bring to mind a moment of genuine gratitude—a person, a memory, or a feeling. Let yourself feel it fully.

- Stay with that feeling for a few minutes. Let it expand. Let it anchor into your body. Repeat a phrase like: "All parts of me are welcome here."

Practicing this regularly helps your mind and heart speak the same language: the language of compassion, curiosity, and connection. That is the space where integration happens.

Reflection Questions:

What parts of you still feel disconnected or rejected? What would it feel like to welcome them in?

_____

_____

_____

_____

When was the last time you truly listened to your heart? What did it say?

_____

_____

_____

_____

What would healing look like if you approached yourself with unconditional acceptance?

_____

_____

_____

_____

Action Step: Shadow Work—A Path to Wholeness

Before You Begin: A Note of Gratitude and Encouragement

Before we dive into the action step, I want to take a moment to honor you. Shadow work isn't easy. It's raw, it's real, and it asks you to look at the parts of yourself you've spent a long time avoiding. But here you are. Still reading. Still showing up. Still choosing to do the inner work that most people never even dare to face.

That alone deserves acknowledgment.

I am so proud of you for making it this far. You've already shown courage by being willing to look deeper, to ask the hard questions, and to get honest with yourself. Shadow work is not about fixing what's broken, it's about remembering the parts of you that got lost along the way. It's not about fixing or labeling anything as wrong. It's about remembering that wholeness includes all of us, even the parts we've tried to hide. It's about compassion, not condemnation. It's about acceptance, not shame. This practice invites self-compassion, courage, and truth. And it can be a profound step in your healing journey.

This next step might stir some discomfort, but I promise it will also open the door to freedom, to clarity, and to a level of self-understanding that creates true transformation.

Take a moment. Breathe deeply.

Ground yourself in the knowing that you are safe to explore all parts of you.

You are supported, and you are ready.

Part 1: Recognize the Judgments

When you look at archetypes you admire, you see your best self. Well, the opposite is true, too. When you judge others in a negative way, often, you're judging the parts of yourself that you may not like. Think of people or groups you've judged. What beliefs, actions, or values trigger something within you? Maybe it's a lifestyle choice, a behavior, or an energy that stirs frustration or resentment. Write them down, honestly and without shame.

Do your best not to judge yourself during this exercise. It's human nature to make judgments. Instead of judging your judgments, allow this exercise to be cathartic.

Judgment is not a flaw. It's often a mirror. Don't judge the judgment. Just let it surface.

Who or what have you judged?

_____

_____

_____

_____

_____

What specifically bothers you about them?

_____

_____

_____

_____

Part 2: Find Yourself in the Mirror

You may enjoy claiming your archetype's special powers, which you might project onto the people you admire. But it may not be comfortable to claim the shadow that you've projected onto someone else. Offer yourself self-compassion as you continue this exercise. Now gently ask yourself: _How am I like this in some way?_ This might be subtle. It doesn't have to be the same behavior, but maybe the same root emotion or fear. The shadow hides in comparison, but it softens in self-awareness.

What does this judgment reflect back to you?

_____

_____

_____

In what ways have you also shown up like this?

_____

_____

_____

Part 3: Explore the Shadow

Your ego has been holding on to these judgments for a reason, oftentimes to draw an imaginary line between the people or groups you judge and yourself. But that imaginary line comes at a cost. It creates a false sense of separation that you are not like them. But the truth is, we all carry light and shadow. Now, look at what the judgment is protecting. What does it give you? And what is it costing you? In the spaces provided, explore why your ego might be holding on to these judgments, and then consider how these judgments are holding you back.

What's the perceived benefit of holding onto this judgment?

_____

_____

_____

_____

How is it holding you back from the person you are becoming?

_____

_____

_____

_____

Part 4: Return to Your True Self

Compassion You Receive

This part is about healing through compassion. First, receive compassion from someone you trust, real or imagined. Call to mind someone from your life who acts, or has acted, as a mentor or guide. They might be a coach, teacher, spiritual figure, or archetype—anyone you see yourself seeking counsel from during a difficult time. Write down the compassionate phrases or words you know this person would say to you.

What would they say to you right now?

_____

_____

_____

_____

_____

Compassion You Give

Next, offer compassion. Think of someone you deeply care about who is struggling, or someone who might seek your wise counsel during times of difficulty. Think of someone who typically respects your opinion and often shares with you in confidence. Imagine that they've come to you after uncovering something about their shadow. Write down compassionate words you might say to them.

What would you say to them if they came to you with the same judgment or fear?

_____

_____

_____

_____

_____

My Compassionate Statement

Now, take both of those voices and weave them into one phrase you can return to—a loving reminder of your wholeness. Pick out keywords from all the phrases you've listed above. Put the phrases into a single statement. For example, if you've listed "You are supported" and "Wrap yourself in love," your statement might be, "May I be supported and wrapped in love."

What compassionate phrase do you most need to hear right now?

_____

_____

_____

_____

_____

Turn it into a statement of love and truth.

_____

_____

_____

_____

_____

Part 5: Reflect & Reintegrate

After you've completed your shadow action step, it's time to reflect on the experience. From your new place of self-compassion and coming back to yourself, think back to the people you initially judged. Does the judgment feel a little less charged now that you can own this similar tendency in yourself? What do you see now from this new perspective? You've uncovered a lot. Take a breath. Now ask yourself:

Does the judgment you began with feel different now?

_____

_____

_____

_____

_____

What truth do you see that you didn't see before?

_____

_____

_____

_____

What part of yourself have you reconnected with today?

_____

_____

_____

_____

This work is not about erasing the shadow. It's about bringing it home. Every judgment, every trigger, is an invitation to come back to your whole self. When you hold space for your shadow, you open space for healing, empathy, and deep transformation.

Chapter Summary: Embracing All of You

Shadow work isn't about fixing what's wrong with you. It's about reclaiming the parts of you that have been waiting to be seen with compassion. In this chapter, you took an honest, courageous look at the places you've judged, rejected, or buried within yourself. You stepped toward those shadows, not to erase them, but to understand them. That is healing.

> *Shadow work isn't about fixing what's wrong with you. It's about reclaiming the parts of you that have been waiting to be seen with compassion.*

Through my own story, those moments when I felt judgment rise watching others make health choices I no longer had the privilege to make, I discovered that what I was really seeing were reflections of my own wounds. My fear. My grief. My sense of powerlessness. Once I was willing to look inward instead of outward, everything changed. The judgment softened. Compassion grew. And my capacity to hold space for others, including clients, loved ones, and even myself, deepened.

The science in this chapter showed that our stress responses, our unconscious reactions, and even our most automatic judgments are not character flaws. They are adaptations. And they can be re-patterned. You've seen how the mind, body, and spirit work together to hold pain, and how they can work together to heal it, too. From Carl Jung's shadow theory to Dr. Sapolsky's research on chronic stress, from the deep wisdom of the heart's intelligence to the practical tools of breathwork and reflection, you now understand what it means to be whole.

Wholeness isn't about perfection. It's about integration.

It's about welcoming the Windsock Guy moments, the hidden fears, the judgments, the truth that's been buried underneath, and the awareness this brings. It's about seeing yourself clearly and loving yourself anyway. You've already begun that process. And that is something to be deeply proud of.

Keep going. There is power in your shadows, wisdom in your wounds, and strength in your softness.

You are not broken.

You are coming back to you.

CHAPTER 7

Releasing & Letting Go: Clearing Space for Growth

Personal Story: A Time When Letting Go Created Space for Something Better

Letting go doesn't always start with a big, dramatic moment. Sometimes, it begins with something as small as a plate. A sponge. A memory. A voice in your head that isn't even yours anymore.

I was around eight years old, standing on a step stool at the kitchen sink, sleeves rolled up, hands already wrinkled from warm, soapy water. Dinner was over. My job had just begun. I had to clear the table, rinse the dishes, load the dishwasher, scrub the pots and pans, wipe down the counters, clean the stove, and make sure the table was spotless. Only then would I be allowed to watch TV, call a friend, or just breathe. But first? Inspection. I remember the sound of the television in the other room. My parents were laughing at whatever show they were watching. Meanwhile, I stood alone in the kitchen, quietly muttering to myself, *You missed a spot again. Hurry up. They're going to come in and check.* It wasn't said aloud, but I could feel it. Their eyes. The pressure. The expectation that everything had to be perfect or done a certain way, and without shortcuts.

It became the way I learned to measure worth: Finish your work. Don't complain. Don't ask for help. Earn your rest.

Fast forward to when I was 15, newly dating the boy who would one day become my husband. We were at his parents' house for dinner. Everyone was gathered around a long table, plates filled, laughter floating easily between them. His parents were still married and obviously in love. He teased his younger sister over dessert. His dad filled glasses with a wink. It felt warm, relaxed, and foreign.

After dinner, everyone casually stood, grabbed their plates, and brought them into the kitchen. But that was it. They just… left them there—pots still on the stove, food cooling on the plates. I looked around, waiting for someone to say, "Let's get this cleaned up." But no one did. They went back to the table with their drinks and kept talking, as if the dishes had disappeared.

I was stunned.

I remember pulling my boyfriend aside and whispering, "Should I go clean that up?"

He looked at me like I had three heads. "No, it's fine. We'll get to it later."

I couldn't relax. My eyes kept darting to the kitchen. My body tensed like a coiled spring. I tried to focus on the conversation, to sip my drink, to laugh at the jokes. But in my head, a different dialogue was playing: *You can't leave a mess. That's lazy. It's disrespectful. It'll dry and be impossible to clean. You're being irresponsible.*

It wasn't just a mess on the counter. It was chaos in my nervous system.

Later, as our relationship deepened, those dishes followed us into our life together. We made an agreement early on that I would cook and he would clean. It seemed fair. But over time, I noticed resentment quietly creeping in. I'd make dinner, we'd eat, and I'd wait. He didn't always rush to clean the kitchen the way I expected. Sometimes he'd wander off. Sometimes he'd leave things until the next morning. And me? I'd be there angrily scrubbing, muttering under my breath, "Why do I have to do everything?"

He never understood why I was so upset. I'd explode over dishes, but it wasn't about the dishes. Not really. It was about the narrative I had been living with for decades. The one that said if something isn't done right away, I had failed. If I rested before the work was done, I was irresponsible. If there was a mess, I was the mess.

He, bless his heart, was the teenager with peanut butter and crackers stashed in his room, always a butter knife crusted with crumbs nearby. He didn't feel the same urgency. And at first, I judged that. But slowly, through my mindset, emotional, and spiritual work, I started to see the difference. He wasn't disrespectful. He wasn't lazy. He just hadn't been conditioned the same way I had.

It wasn't about the dishes at all. It was about the programming.

Once I realized that, everything shifted. I began to see how much energy I spent carrying old expectations. The way I'd unconsciously force the same pressure onto my husband or kids, without even realizing I was doing it. The way I'd grit my teeth and clean up out of obligation, then quietly boil with resentment, punishing them for my unspoken rules.

I remember one night after dinner with my family, I caught myself standing in the kitchen, on autopilot, reaching for the sponge while everyone else sat laughing in the next room. And I paused. I heard that old voice whisper, *You have to clean this before you can sit down.* But then, another voice rose up. One that was new. Softer. Mine.

No, you don't. The dishes can wait. This moment can't.

I let go of the sponge. I wiped my hands. And I walked into the living room and sat down.

That was the beginning of my freedom.

It didn't happen all at once. I still catch myself sometimes, jumping up too soon, cleaning without even thinking. But now I can smile at it. I can breathe through it. I can see it for what it is—not a crisis, but a choice. And I choose presence. I choose peace. Letting go isn't always dramatic. Sometimes, it's just choosing joy over obligation. Connection over control. Yourself over your programming.

> Letting go isn't always dramatic. Sometimes, it's just choosing joy over obligation.

Sometimes, what starts with a sink full of dishes leads you back home.

The Emotional Weight of Holding On: What Science Says About Stress and Trauma Storage

Letting go wasn't something I was taught. It certainly wasn't something I saw modeled.

In my childhood home, things had to be done a certain way, at a certain time, and to a certain standard. I had responsibilities, chores, and expectations, and they weren't negotiable. There was no room for "later," no one saying, "It's okay if that's not perfect." I learned early that my worth was wrapped up in how much I could accomplish and how well I followed the rules. And if I didn't? There were consequences. Not just reprimands, but deep, unspoken tension that filled the room. The withdrawal of affection. The weight of disapproval.

Fast forward decades later, and I found myself in my own home— married, a mother, and a high-pressure vice president of engineering— healing from chronic illness and still stuck in that same loop. That same pressure. That same voice in my head that said, *Do more. Be more. Get it all right.* Even after all the growth, all the work, and all the healing I had done, I still found myself losing peace over something as simple as the dishes in the sink after dinner.

But it was never really about the dishes.

It was about the way my nervous system had been conditioned to stay alert, to anticipate judgment, and to avoid conflict by staying ahead of any potential problem. My husband and I had very different upbringings. He didn't see dishes as a big deal. I saw them as unfinished business, a symbol of failing to meet the mark. If something was left undone, I couldn't relax. I couldn't settle. I couldn't enjoy the moment because my body didn't feel safe unless everything was in order.

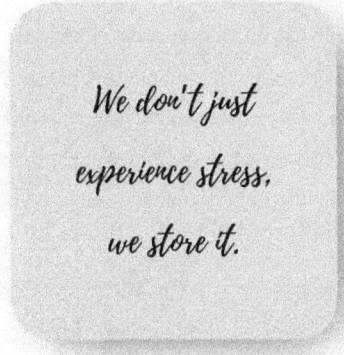

We don't just experience stress, we store it.

In *The Body Keeps the Score*, Dr. Bessel van der Kolk explains how trauma, big or small, even the subtle kind that comes from growing up in high-pressure environments, doesn't just live in our thoughts. It lives in our bodies. Our shoulders hunch. Our stomachs tighten. Our breath becomes shallow. We clench, grip, and hold, physically mirroring what we're afraid to let go of emotionally. And over time, this creates a cascade of symptoms: fatigue, brain fog, pain, tension, and chronic illness. I didn't just feel resentment. I held it in my body.

And according to Dr. Robert Sapolsky's research, when we're under chronic stress, cortisol stays elevated. This long-term stress hormone disrupts the immune system, digestion, and memory, and even leads to inflammation and autoimmune conditions. His book, *Why Zebras Don't Get Ulcers*, shows that while animals can quickly move out of a stress response, we humans often stay stuck in it, thinking, worrying, and over-processing every thought, emotion, and reaction. We don't just experience stress—we store it. I lived all of that. My body paid the price for years of internalized pressure and unprocessed emotion.

There was a time when I thought I just needed to manage my to-do list better. Now, I know that what I really needed was to stop carrying so much.

To stop gripping so tightly to the beliefs and expectations that were never truly mine to begin with. I saw this so clearly once I started to slow down—the anxiety in my chest when the kitchen wasn't clean, the tension in my jaw when I felt unappreciated, the exhaustion that came from constantly trying to meet invisible expectations. I wasn't just tired. I was holding too much.

And here's the powerful part. Our brains are capable of change.

According to Dr. Norman Doidge and Dr. Michael Merzenich, the brain is neuroplastic. That means it rewires based on repeated thought patterns and behaviors. The more we cling to old stories, the stronger those neural pathways become. But when we begin to release those beliefs, create space, and practice something new, we form new pathways. We create new responses. We give ourselves a new reality.

But this isn't just a mental process. True transformation involves all parts of you.

This wasn't just about rewiring my mindset. It was about retraining my entire system, mind, body, and spirit. I had to notice the thoughts that sounded like truth but were really just old programming, such as *If I don't do it all, I'm not doing enough,* or *I'm only lovable if I'm useful,* and replace them with thoughts that actually supported me. I began using breathwork, grounding techniques, and slow movement to help my body feel safe when I chose rest. I let my body know that it was okay to pause. Okay to breathe. I remembered that I am not here to prove myself. I am here to be myself. Letting go became a spiritual act, a way of clearing the clutter in my soul so that I could reconnect with joy, creativity, and presence.

Begin to notice the stories you've been telling yourself about what you have to do, who you have to be, and why rest or joy feels unsafe. The thoughts we repeat become our truth, but they don't have to stay that way. Your body is your messenger. It will always tell you when something is ready to be released. Through breathwork, movement, and somatic practices, we signal to the nervous system that it's safe to relax and let go.

Spiritually, holding on creates energetic clutter. It disconnects us from the present and dims our connection to intuition and peace. Letting go is an act of trust. It says, *I no longer need to carry what isn't mine.* It opens space for grace to flow in.

Letting go didn't come in one big moment. It came in small moments, like the night I left the dishes in the sink so I could laugh with my husband. Or the morning I chose to meditate instead of checking one more thing off the list. It came when I started listening to what my body was saying instead of what my conditioning was screaming. It came when I realized that my nervous system deserved rest—that I didn't have to earn peace, I could just choose it. When I finally stopped trying to control every detail, something beautiful happened. I created space. Space for stillness. Space for connection. Space for healing. And in that space, I found myself again.

Letting go is not a one-time event. It's a daily practice. It's choosing to soften your grip, to breathe a little deeper, and to believe that you are worthy of peace, even if the dishes aren't done.

Reflection Questions:

What are you holding onto, emotionally, physically, or energetically, that is no longer serving you?

_____

_____

_____

_____

How does your body respond when you're carrying too much? Where do you feel it?

_____

_____

_____

_____

What would it feel like to soften your grip and trust that letting go will make room for something better?

_____

_____

_____

_____

How the Past Impacts Your Present Choices and the Energetic Impact of Clutter, Relationships, and Old Identities

Letting go is never just about the dishes.

For so many of us, our current struggles with boundaries, relationships, health, or even clutter are not just surface-level issues. They are echoes of the past. Patterns we absorbed without question. Roles we learned to play. Stories we were taught to believe about who we needed to be in order to feel safe, worthy, or loved.

What I've come to understand is that these old identities become energetic clutter: the perfectionism, the pressure, the caretaking, the overthinking, the need to do everything yourself because you are afraid no one else will show up for you. This energy lingers in our nervous system, in our behaviors, in our homes, and in the way we show up in relationships.

Our bodies carry the memory of these roles. You might find yourself cleaning obsessively after a dinner party, not because you truly want to, but because deep down, rest does not feel safe unless everything is done. Or maybe you avoid conflict because your nervous system learned early on that speaking up led to punishment, tension, or abandonment. These behaviors are not random. They are wired into the nervous system as protective patterns.

And here's the thing: your nervous system is doing its job. It's trying to keep you safe based on what it's learned. But what kept you safe back then may be keeping you stuck now.

This is where Dr. Stephen Porges's Polyvagal Theory comes in. His research shows that the vagus nerve plays a key role in how our bodies interpret and respond to safety and threat. This nerve runs from the brainstem through the chest and gut and acts as a communication highway between the brain and the body. When we experience stress or emotional overwhelm, the vagus nerve helps regulate how we respond. It determines whether we stay calm and connected, or shift into fight, flight, or shutdown. It helps regulate our emotional state and our ability to connect with others. When we are in chronic states of stress, whether physical, emotional, or spiritual, the vagus nerve signals the body to stay in survival mode.

This is why nervous system regulation is such a core piece of healing. The vagus nerve is part of the parasympathetic nervous system, the branch responsible for rest, repair, and healing. When it is activated through practices like breathwork, meditation, humming, chanting, or grounding, it signals to the body that we are safe. This helps reduce cortisol, regulate the heartbeat, calm the mind, and return the nervous system to a more balanced state.

Studies have shown that high vagal tone, which reflects strong vagus nerve function, is associated with greater emotional resilience, stronger

immune function, and better stress
management. On the other hand, a
chronically activated stress response,
often the result of trauma or unprocessed
emotion, can keep the vagus nerve in a
suppressed state. This can lead to
symptoms like anxiety, fatigue, tension,
and emotional reactivity.

> *We don't just carry physical clutter. We carry emotional clutter. Mental clutter. Energetic clutter.*

As we learned earlier, HRV is a key
marker of vagus nerve health. It measures the variation in time between
heartbeats. A higher HRV indicates a more flexible nervous system that can
quickly adapt to stress and return to balance. According to a meta-analysis
by Thayer and colleagues in 2012, individuals with a higher HRV are more
emotionally stable and resilient, while those with a lower HRV are more
prone to anxiety and depressive symptoms. Practices like deep breathing,
gentle movement, meditation, or even humming can help stimulate the vagus
nerve and move the body from *fight-or-flight* to *rest-and-digest*. That's where
clarity returns. That's where healing becomes possible. That's where you
begin to feel like yourself again.

I've felt it in my own body. Those moments when resentment builds,
when I feel the compulsion to do everything—to clean up before the last bite
has even been taken, to anticipate every need before it's voiced—that's not
my truth speaking. That's old conditioning. That's the scared little girl who
thought her worth was measured in how much she could hold for everyone
else.

We don't just carry physical clutter. We carry emotional clutter. Mental
clutter. Energetic clutter. And it accumulates slowly: the expectations,
perfectionism, fear of letting people down, shame around needing help, and
pressure to do it all. This is why clearing emotional, mental, and energetic
clutter is such an important part of nervous system regulation. When we
release old patterns, outdated beliefs, and unresolved emotional weight, we
create space. Not just space in our schedule or our home, but space in the
nervous system. Space for breath. Space for rest. Space for possibility.

And it is not just about releasing physical things. Sometimes, what we need to let go of is an identity. The identity of the fixer. The responsible one. The one who holds it all together. The one who has to be strong for everyone else. The truth is, your body remembers even when your mind does not. If your nervous system still lives in a past story, your present-day choices will reflect that. You may feel stuck or overwhelmed, not because you lack willpower, but because your nervous system is trying to protect you based on outdated information. Sometimes it means setting down the need to control every detail, or acknowledging that your nervous system is still reacting to a past that isn't happening anymore. These identities may have once helped us survive, but they are not required for us to thrive.

When we combine nervous system practices like deep breathing with emotional and spiritual awareness, we begin to rewire those old stories. We move from reactivity to intentionality. From survival to creation. From constriction to expansion.

Letting go is not just a release. It is an energetic shift. It is a sacred clearing of the things that no longer serve the person you are becoming. And it creates the spaciousness for healing, joy, and transformation to take root. When you clear emotional and energetic clutter, you create space. Space to breathe. Space to rest. Space for joy. Space to receive support. And in that space, your nervous system begins to learn something new: *I don't have to hold it all anymore.*

This is why I integrate nervous system regulation into all my healing work. Because without safety in the body, true release can't happen. You have to feel safe enough to let go.

Reflection Questions:

Where in your life are you still carrying emotional, mental, or energetic clutter from a past identity or experience?

_____

_____

_____

_____

How does your nervous system signal that something is unresolved? What does it feel like in your body?

_____

_____

_____

_____

What would it feel like to let something go, not because it's wrong or bad, but because it's simply no longer yours to carry?

_____

_____

_____

_____

The Power of Rituals, Energy Clearing, and Intentional Release

Letting go is not just something you do with your mind or a decision you make in your head. It's something you do with your energy. With your body. With your breath. It's a change in how we carry ourselves and a choice to clear space mentally, emotionally, and spiritually so that something new can take root. It's one thing to think, *I'm releasing this,* but it's another to actually feel the weight of it leave your system.

We all carry things that no longer serve us, including thoughts, emotions, responsibilities, stories, patterns, and even relationships. And sometimes, the only way to release them is to pause long enough to notice they're still there. That's where ritual and intention come in. Whether it's through meditation, movement, or simply taking a breath with presence, these small acts create big shifts.

Rituals are sacred practices that speak directly to your subconscious and your spirit. They give your nervous system a cue. They create closure. They signal to your energy field that something has shifted. Whether it's lighting a candle, breathing with intention, smudging your space, or writing something down and then burning it, ritual turns an idea into a felt experience.

Science supports this deeply spiritual practice. Research from Dr. Sara Lazar at Harvard shows that consistent meditation thickens the prefrontal cortex, the part of your brain responsible for focus, decision-making, and emotional regulation (2005). Just eight weeks of practice has been shown to improve attention, reduce reactivity, and support clearer thinking. And it goes further. Dr. Richard Davidson found that meditation also reduces cortisol, your stress hormone, and strengthens immune function (2003). So when we pause for ritual or mindfulness, we're not just centering ourselves, we're physically shifting how our brain and body respond to stress.

That's why mindfulness practices are foundational in my coaching. They reconnect us to ourselves. They help us release what's been weighing us down and create clarity where confusion once lived. A simple five-minute practice can change the way your day unfolds. It can bring you out of reaction and back into rhythm with your body, your purpose, and your truth.

Another way we access healing is through flow. Dr. Mihaly Csikszentmihalyi's work on flow state shows us that being fully immersed in what we love allows our brain to move out of resistance and into effortless presence. Flow creates alignment. When you are in flow, whether it's journaling, meditating, dancing, painting, hiking, running, building, or problem-solving, you're not forcing release; you're allowing it. And in that space, we are in a state of effortless alignment. That's when creativity, intuition, and healing can really move.

Spiritually speaking, this all connects to energy. Dr. Deepak Chopra's research in quantum healing explains how our consciousness, intentions, and thoughts influence our physical and emotional health. He says that consciousness and intention can shift our energy field and even influence the healing of our physical bodies. That's powerful. When we engage in energy-clearing rituals, through breathwork, guided meditation, journaling, or simply stepping into nature with awareness, we're not just "feeling better." We're shifting the frequency at which we're operating. We're tuning in to the part of us that already knows what's aligned and what needs to be released. And I've seen it in my own life. When I set clear intentions and release the clutter, mental, emotional, and spiritual, I feel more aligned. My body responds. My heart opens. I come back to myself.

Chopra's work, along with Dr. Bruce Lipton's research on epigenetics, affirms that our beliefs, habits, and even emotions influence gene expression. That means your thoughts don't just stay in your head. Your thoughts, beliefs, and energy all influence your body. They ripple into your cells. They shape your health. When you release old beliefs through ritual or spiritual practice, you're not just shifting your mindset, you're shifting your biology. And it's not just about healing the past. It's about creating space for what's next. I've learned that release creates room for growth. For breath. For vision. When you let go of what no longer fits, you can begin to receive what's aligned.

This isn't just about healing. It's about clearing. When we release emotional baggage, mental clutter, or even energetic tension, we begin to feel more connected to our purpose. We trust ourselves more. We start to live and lead from clarity, not reaction. And just like physical clutter, emotional and energetic clutter can pile up when we're not paying attention. Letting go becomes the invitation to come back to yourself. To return to what matters. To breathe deeper, think clearly, and feel more like yourself.

Here's a simple release ritual I love:

- Find a safe space where you feel relaxed. This could be in your home, outside, or even a favorite place.

- If you'd like, light a candle. Then, set the intention to let go of what's weighing you down.

- Write down what you're ready to release: a belief, a pattern, a story that no longer serves you. Freely write. Don't hold back! Write exactly what you may not want to say or anyone to see or hear.

- Read it out loud, if it's safe to do so, or read it back to yourself. Feel it in your body.

- Then tear it up, shred it, or burn it (safely) as a symbolic act of release.

- Place your hands over your heart. Breathe deeply. Whisper a phrase of freedom: "I release this with love. I make space for what is meant for me."

This isn't about perfection. It's about permission. To release. To rise. To come back to the truth of who you are.

Reflection Questions:

What are you holding onto that is no longer aligned with who you are becoming? (This could be a belief, a pattern, an identity, or an old story. Let yourself be honest and gentle.)

_____

_____

_____

_____

What does your body feel like when you're carrying emotional, mental, or energetic weight? (Where do you feel it? What signals does your body give you when it's time to let go?)

_____

_____

_____

_____

What small but intentional practice could you use to reset, release, and reconnect with yourself? (Maybe it's breathwork, a walk in nature, journaling, or a daily pause to check in.)

_____

_____

_____

Action Step: Releasing With Purpose—Moving From Clutter to Clarity

By now, you've explored the stories, beliefs, and patterns that have been taking up space in your body, your energy, and your life. You've looked at the emotional clutter and the ways your nervous system is still holding onto a past that isn't happening anymore.

Let's turn this awareness into intentional momentum.

This practice is grounded in the principles of Motivational Interviewing, or MI, a compassionate, client-centered approach designed to guide people through ambivalence and toward meaningful change. At its core, MI is not about fixing. It's about uncovering the truth that's already within you.

We're going to bring this into your journey right now.

Take a moment. Get still. Breathe.

Now answer these questions with honesty, curiosity, and gentleness. Write freely and without judgment.

What is one change you are ready to make, not because you "should," but because your soul is calling for it? (Think of something that feels aligned with the person you are becoming. This could be a habit, a boundary, a mindset, or a way of relating to yourself or others.)

_____

_____

_____

_____

Why is this change deeply important to you right now? (Not for anyone else. Not for approval or validation. Why does this matter for you, your healing, and your happiness?)

_____

_____

_____

_____

What is one small, doable step you can take today to move in that direction? (Not the entire path. Just the first step. Something you can do in the next 24 hours to shift energy, clear space, or take aligned action.)

_____

_____

_____

_____

This isn't about overhauling your life overnight. It's about planting a seed of intention. One step at a time. One breath at a time. When you show your nervous system that change is safe and aligned, you begin to build new patterns from a place of peace, not pressure. Let this be your gentle reset. A chance to move from clutter to clarity, from holding on to opening up, from stuck to spacious.

You are ready.

Chapter Summary: Letting Go to Let Life In

Letting go is not just an act, it's a practice. A deep breath. A conscious choice. A quiet revolution inside the nervous system. For years, I believed letting go meant giving up, being careless, or not honoring my responsibilities. But I've learned that true letting go is an act of love. It's choosing presence over pressure, alignment over obligation, and peace over perfection.

> *What started as a story about dishes really became a story about identity, control, and deep emotional clutter.*

What started as a story about dishes really became a story about identity, control, and deep emotional clutter. The voice that told me to clean up before I could rest wasn't just about a chore. It was about how I had been taught to earn rest, prove my worth, and hold everything together. But I know now, rest is not a reward. Peace is not a privilege. And I am not here to be a machine.

You've explored how the body stores emotion, how the nervous system holds onto old roles and narratives long after they've expired, and how spiritual and scientific practices, from breathwork and meditation to intention-setting and ritual, help us clear space on every level. Letting go isn't one big moment. It's a thousand small choices. To pause instead of push. To breathe instead of brace. To say, "I matter too," and then live like it's true. Letting go doesn't mean you lose who you are. It means you make room for who you've been becoming all along.

You are not behind. You are not broken. You are shedding what no longer serves so that you can fully return to yourself—the whole, wise, and worthy version of you that's been waiting underneath all the noise.

Let this chapter be a permission slip.

To pause. To exhale. To release what is no longer yours to carry.

You're not just letting go. You're coming home.

Thriving in Alignment: Living Your Mission Me 2.0

CHAPTER 8

The Power of Presence: Mastering the Present Moment

Personal Story: A Personal Experience of Being Fully Present That Led to Clarity

Letting go and reclaiming my presence didn't begin with mindfulness exercises or meditation. It began with grief. And before that, it began with years of silence.

When I was young, it was just me and my dad. We weren't perfect, but we had each other. After my parents' divorce, we moved into a beautiful home on a lake, a fresh start, a rebuild, just the two of us. There was comfort in our rhythm. I helped out, but it felt like we were a team. I felt seen, valued, and deeply connected to him. And then *she* entered our lives.

My stepmother brought with her a new set of expectations, roles, and energy. Slowly, everything changed. It wasn't immediate, but it was undeniable. The balance tipped, and I fell to the bottom. What had once felt like a partnership became a hierarchy, and I was no longer at the table.

Growing up with her, I often felt like Cinderella—not the kind with a magical fairy godmother, but the version scrubbing floors, trying not to cry, and holding in all the words she didn't dare say out loud. I cleaned the house, helped prepare meals, and did the dishes. I wasn't invited to rest. My stepmother did her own laundry and cleaned her room, and my much younger stepsister didn't have to lift a finger. She got to be a child. I felt like the *help*.

> *I thought if I just worked hard enough and kept the peace, maybe I'd be accepted.*

And yet, I stayed quiet. I learned to stay small, avoid confrontation, and prove my value by doing. I thought if I just worked hard enough and kept the peace, maybe I'd be accepted. Maybe I'd be seen again.

But I wasn't. And that ache stayed with me through every chapter that followed. It showed up in subtle ways—how I overachieved, how I overextended, how I said yes when I meant no. It whispered in the background whenever I felt unseen in a room, unheard in a conversation, or unappreciated in my efforts. I became the person who did everything for everyone, not just because I was capable, but because somewhere inside, I still believed I had to earn my place. Even in leadership roles, even in love, even in motherhood, I carried the shadow of that younger self, still trying to scrub away my unworthiness like I used to scrub the kitchen floor.

It wasn't until I gave myself permission to pause, to truly be with the moment instead of performing in it, that I began to unravel the lies. I started asking myself better questions—not *What else can I do?* but *What do I actually need?* Not *How can I fix this?* but *What would it feel like to just be?*

That shift changed everything. Presence wasn't a performance. It was a homecoming, a return to a version of myself that didn't need to prove, push, or earn her way back to love. She simply had to show up.

When I was 16, after a confrontation, I moved out and went to live with my mom. I lived with her and my half-siblings, three very young children, and her husband in a small mobile home. Most people would've assumed I'd choose the big house on the lake. But that little trailer brought me something more important: peace. For the first time in years, I could breathe. Even taking care of the baby and toddlers while my mom worked nights waitressing, I felt more at home. There was no pretense, no judgment. Just love, chaos, and room to be myself.

That decision was the first time I chose presence, even if I didn't know to call it that yet. It was the first time I realized I didn't have to stay where I wasn't valued. But the wounds followed me. I spent years carrying the weight of what I'd experienced—the conditioning, the silence, the resentment I never spoke.

And yet, in adulthood, something shifted between my stepmother and me. As soon as we no longer shared a household, the tension softened. We found a way to meet as two women, not just as stepmother and stepdaughter. She became my confidant. We could talk for hours about my dad, her daughter, work, life, and things only we understood. We traveled together, floated in the pool with drinks in hand on her "adults only" floats, and just *were*. Quiet moments cross-stitching or playing cards for hours reminded me that even in the complicated, there can be connection. She was the Matron of Honor at my wedding. My stepmother. My best friend. We still had our barriers, but we also had real closeness, a bond formed through years of navigating each other's edges. That relationship, layered as it was, taught me that sometimes the love we feel doesn't erase the pain, and the pain doesn't erase the love. Both can exist. And I carry that truth with me always. And when she passed suddenly in a car accident, I didn't just grieve what was lost. I grieved the version of us that was filled with that love and connection.

After her death, something else happened, too. With her gone, it was as if a heavy veil had been lifted. My father and I quickly found our way back to each other. There was space again. The barrier between us was no longer there, physically or emotionally. Instead of just being together out of family obligation, there was an openness that had been smothered for so long. We had long, honest conversations, and for the first time in a long time, I felt him meet me with truth and vulnerability. We spoke openly about the past. He saw things he hadn't seen before. I forgave things I hadn't yet acknowledged. Our connection deepened in a way that only grief seems to allow.

But the family tension didn't end there.

In the aftermath of her death, her side of the family turned on him, and then on me. They blamed him for the accident. They

It wasn't until the noise stopped, the voices, the conflict, the attempts to manage everyone else's pain, that I truly learned the power of presence.

harassed him. And when he died unexpectedly three years later, the grief came with chaos: texts, social media posts, even vandalism at his grave. Their hostility had no boundaries. I had to get a restraining order. I blocked every account. I shut the door. It was the only way to protect my peace.

For years, I had tried to be the one to keep the family together, the peacemaker, the bridge, the oldest child holding everyone else's pieces, attending everything out of obligation and pretending to want to be there. But eventually, I saw it for what it was: a losing battle rooted in a belief that I had to earn love through effort and that I had to fix what was never mine to repair. Why did I still have hope? Because I was still that little girl who once believed she had to do everything just to be enough. But clarity came when I finally stopped chasing approval and sat still long enough to listen to myself.

It wasn't until the noise stopped—the voices, the conflict, the attempts to manage everyone else's pain—that I truly learned the power of presence. In stillness, I heard the truth: I didn't need to keep proving anything. I didn't need to keep performing. I was worthy of peace, even if the people I once tried to please never saw me.

Presence came in quiet waves, like at his gravesite, staring at the headstone carved with a New England winter scene of a lighthouse and a snowman, a tribute to two lives that were anything but simple. It came in moments when I didn't have to explain, justify, or apologize for who I was. It came when I stopped trying to hold all the pieces together and finally let them fall.

Now, presence is the way I return to myself.

It's how I remember who I am, not who I was told to be. It's how I hold space for others without losing myself. And it's how I continue healing—not by rewriting the past, but by choosing to live fully in the present.

The Neuroscience of Mindfulness: How Presence Shifts Your Reality

Presence is more than a buzzword. Presence isn't just a practice. It's a lifeline. When life feels chaotic, presence is how we come back home to ourselves. It's how we access clarity, calm, and connection. But presence isn't always easy, especially when your nervous system has spent years bracing for impact. I learned that the hard way. After a childhood spent trying to earn my worth through responsibility, performance, and peacekeeping, my body had internalized stress as a baseline. My mind was always scanning. My breath was shallow. I didn't even realize I was holding my shoulders up by my ears most of the time. It's a physiological experience, an emotional recalibration, and a spiritual return. And it shifts your entire reality, because it shifts the way you perceive and respond to the world around you.

I didn't learn presence from a textbook. I learned it standing in hospital rooms, staring at machines, wondering how to hold onto time that was already slipping away. When my father was in his final days, all the noise of the past—resentments, regret, roles—faded into the background. What remained was presence. The quiet knowing that there was nothing else to do but *be there*. No fixing. No proving. Just being. Those moments stripped away everything but the truth. And that is where presence lives.

When we are present, we stop replaying the past and rehearsing the future. We drop into the only place transformation can truly happen: right now.

Dr. Sara Lazar discovered something remarkable. Mindfulness literally changes the brain. Her studies showed that consistent mindfulness practice increases gray matter in the prefrontal cortex and decreases the size of the amygdala, which controls fear and reactivity. MRI scans reveal that meditation thickens the prefrontal cortex, the part of the brain responsible for focus, decision-making, and emotional regulation. Just eight weeks of daily practice creates measurable changes that improve mental clarity, reduce reactivity, and increase our ability to stay grounded when life feels overwhelming. When you are truly present, you interrupt the habitual thought patterns that drive stress, fear, and distraction. You shift from autopilot to awareness. And that changes everything.

When you are truly present, you interrupt the habitual thought patterns that drive stress, fear, and distraction.

This isn't just theoretical. It's life-changing for anyone who has lived in survival mode—for those of us who have had to walk on eggshells, who learned to scan the room for safety, who carried the weight of perfectionism or pain for too long.

Even after years of healing, I would still find myself running through mental to-do lists while brushing my teeth, worrying about everyone else's needs while completely ignoring my own, or replaying old conversations while pretending to relax. I was present for everyone except myself. But then I began to notice the moments that felt different.

When I started practicing presence, just noticing my breath, pausing before reacting, and choosing to feel instead of flee, I could feel those shifts. The noise in my mind softened. My nervous system no longer treated rest as a threat. I could hear myself again. And more importantly, I could trust myself again.

This was true when I sat in the stillness after my father's funeral, hand resting on the carved stone that marked the place where the chaos finally stopped, or when I left the dishes in the sink and chose laughter in the next room instead. These moments weren't about meditation or mindfulness apps.

They were about presence in real life, choosing to be right there, even when it was hard. Even when it hurt. Even when it felt unfamiliar.

That was where the healing began.

Presence is more than a mental exercise. It is felt in the body. When you're truly present, your breath deepens, your heart rate slows, and your muscles relax. Your body gets the message that it is safe. But if you've lived in environments where unpredictability was the norm, your nervous system may be stuck in overdrive. I know mine was. Even in peaceful settings, my body didn't always believe it was safe. Presence retrained that belief. Breathwork, grounding practices, and slow movement all became ways I taught my body it didn't have to keep bracing for the next blow. This is where practices like mindful breathing and heart coherence come in. Even just five slow breaths can activate the parasympathetic nervous system, lower cortisol, and create measurable shifts in HRV, a key marker of resilience and emotional balance. Spiritually, presence is a sacred homecoming. It's not about escaping. It's about arriving.

The flow state is a perfect example. In flow, your brain enters a state of relaxed alertness. Time slows down, creativity increases, and you perform at your highest potential. Whether you're dancing, writing, working on a project, or walking in nature, when you're fully present, you're aligned with your internal rhythm. You aren't chasing time. You're inhabiting it.

So much of our suffering comes from being somewhere else. We get stuck in past pain or rehearsing future fears, trying to rewrite what has already happened or control what hasn't. Presence invites us to release the illusion of control and come back to what is real, right now. This is where flow happens. Dr. Mihaly Csikszentmihalyi's research shows us that when we are immersed in the moment, we access our highest levels of creativity, intuition, and ease. We don't have to force healing. We allow it.

For me, flow began showing up in small moments: journaling while the house was quiet, walking barefoot on the earth, feeling the sunlight through the kitchen window. These weren't escape routes. They were return paths.

They reminded me who I was under the armor. They reminded me that I didn't need to be anywhere else but here.

This is where presence becomes healing. When you are present, your thoughts slow down. You stop looping in stories about the past or fears about the future. This allows your nervous system to shift from hypervigilance to calm awareness. That shift literally rewires your brain. Through neuro-plasticity, your brain builds new neural pathways that favor peace over panic and focus over frenzy. Over time, being present becomes your default. The body feels safe in the now. Chronic stress and reactivity keep cortisol levels high, which weakens immunity and increases inflammation. But presence, through breath, stillness, or movement, activates the parasympathetic nervous system by telling the body it's safe. Muscles release. The breath deepens. The immune system strengthens. It's not just a feeling. It's a biological reset.

Spiritually, presence is where you meet your true self. Not the version shaped by others' expectations or conditioned by past pain, but the core of who you are. When you are present, you become attuned to inner wisdom. You hear your intuition more clearly. You recognize what matters most. Presence is the doorway to purpose. It is the place where your soul can speak.

You don't have to wait until the chaos stops to find presence. You can choose it now, in the small cracks of your day, the moments you pause before reacting, and the seconds where you let yourself feel instead of fix. This isn't about being perfect. It's about being real. It's about reclaiming your attention and your energy. When you bring your presence back to this moment, you bring your power with it.

For me, presence came in the quiet moments I used to avoid—the long walks, the breath between tears, the nights I stared at the stars instead of a screen. It was in those spaces that I realized my reality was not shaped by what happened to me, but by how I chose to meet it. Presence shifts your reality because it brings you back to the only place change is possible: this moment, the here and now. And every time you return to the moment, you reclaim your power to respond instead of react, create instead of repeat, and be instead of perform.

Presence shifts your reality because it brings you back to the only place change is possible: this moment, the here and now.

Reflection Questions:

When was the last time you felt truly present—without performing, planning, or thinking ahead—just fully here? What did it feel like in your body?

_____

_____

_____

_____

What situations or relationships pull you out of presence most often, and why?

_____

_____

_____

_____

What would change in your life if you made presence your daily practice?

_____

_____

_____

_____

What simple practice could you begin today to bring your attention back to the moment, even if just for a breath?

_____

_____

_____

_____

How Past and Future Thinking Create Anxiety and Block Intuition

Anxiety doesn't always show up as panic. Sometimes, it shows up as overthinking, over-preparing, or overdoing. It disguises itself as productivity, responsibility, and planning. But underneath it all, it's fear. And most of that fear is rooted in the past or projected into the future. We try to protect ourselves from pain we've already felt. We replay moments where we felt small, unseen, or unsafe. We try to control what hasn't happened yet, so we never feel that way again. The problem is, we aren't

Anxiety doesn't always show up as panic. Sometimes, it shows up as overthinking, over-preparing, or overdoing.

meant to live in those places. And when we do, we disconnect from the only moment that holds power: the present.

I've lived in both time zones. Past-me would lie awake at night, replaying conversations, wondering if I said the wrong thing, if I could have done more, been more. Future-me made endless to-do lists, worried about what might go wrong, braced for disaster that never came. In both places, I was exhausted. My nervous system didn't know the difference between memory and imagination. My body responded with the same tension, the same shallow breath, the same fatigue. I was surviving in alert mode, and I couldn't hear anything but the noise in my head.

That's the thing. When we live in the past or the future, we block our own guidance. We block our intuition. Intuition speaks in the quiet, in the now. It's that soft whisper of knowing that can't get through when your mind is busy replaying or predicting.

Science supports this, too. Dr. Robert Sapolsky's work shows that the body reacts to perceived threats the same way it reacts to real ones. The stress hormone cortisol floods the system whether you're facing danger or just imagining it. Chronic stress keeps you stuck in survival mode. It dulls the prefrontal cortex, the part of your brain responsible for insight and decision-making. That's why intuition gets buried under stress. You're not broken, you're overloaded. And it's not just the mind. The body remembers. Past thinking lives in our shoulders, our jaw, and our chest. Future thinking lives in our gut, the racing heart, and the clenching we can't quite explain. Spiritually, both pull us away from alignment. When we ruminate or anticipate, we disconnect from our higher self, clarity, and trust.

The answer isn't to ignore the past or avoid the future. It's to meet them with presence. To notice when you've left the moment and gently return. That's how intuition begins to rise. That's how anxiety begins to soften. It's not about stopping thoughts. It's about anchoring yourself in what is real, what is now, and allowing that to be enough.

Reflection Questions:

When your mind pulls you to the past, what patterns do you notice? What emotions live there?

_____

_____

_____

_____

When you worry about the future, what are you afraid might happen? How does your body respond?

_____

_____

_____

_____

What helps you return to the present moment when you feel anxious or overwhelmed?

_____

_____

_____

_____

The Role of Meditation, Somatic Awareness, and Movement in Deepening Presence

Healing doesn't just happen in the mind. It lives in the body. It pulses through your breath. It speaks in your energy. That's why the journey to presence is not only about thoughts, but about movement, rhythm, stillness, and flow. For me, deepening awareness meant learning to listen to all parts of myself—not just my mind, but my body's signals and my spirit's quiet voice. To feel instead of flee. To soften instead of brace. To stay present with what was moving through me rather than rush to fix it.

When I started to move again after being sick, it wasn't about exercise. It was about reconnecting. I didn't need a rigid fitness routine. I needed to *feel safe* in my body again. I needed to stretch where fear had taken root. I needed to dance with what had been stuck. Whether it was moving through sun salutations, dancing freely in the kitchen, or sitting in quiet meditation, these were the practices that reminded me I was still here. Still whole. Still becoming. They brought me back to myself.

In *The Body Keeps the Score*, Dr. Bessel van der Kolk explains how trauma is stored in the body as tension, inflammation, or shutdown. He found that practices like yoga and somatic movement help release that stored trauma by accessing the nervous system directly. It's not enough to talk about your pain. Your body has to feel safe enough to let it go. That's where mindful movement becomes medicine. This is why practices like yoga and intuitive movement are so powerful. They help the body process what words cannot. And you don't need to be flexible or fit. You just need to be willing to listen. Willing to stay with what arises. Willing to give your body the attention it's been waiting for.

From a physiological perspective, movement helps regulate the nervous system. Research from Harvard Medical School shows that slow, meditative movement practices like Tai Chi and Qigong significantly reduce cortisol levels and improve immune function. They help bring the nervous system back into balance by gently inviting us to slow down, tune in, and release. That's what healing requires—not force, but permission. Not more doing, but deeper being. When we move with intention, we aren't just stretching muscles. We are reorganizing energy. We are clearing space for clarity to enter.

> *Meditation became one of the most powerful ways I accessed presence, not by escaping my body, but by dropping into it.*

Meditation became one of the most powerful ways I accessed presence, not by escaping my body, but by dropping into it. The type of meditation I guide isn't about silencing thoughts. It's about building awareness of how your body feels, how your breath moves, and what emotions are waiting beneath the surface. I use body-based cues, breath awareness, and grounding to help others feel safe enough to be still. When we combine mindfulness with somatic processing, we don't just calm the mind, we give the body what it's been asking for: acknowledgment and release.

Breathwork, too, is a direct pathway to presence. It's portable. It's free. And it's incredibly effective. Deep breathing stimulates the vagus nerve and shifts the body into parasympathetic mode, the rest and heal state. Even five minutes a day can recalibrate your stress response and bring you back to the present.

But presence isn't just physical. It's energetic.

The HeartMath Institute found that the heart sends more electrical signals to the brain than the brain sends to the heart. When you regulate your heart rhythm through breath and gratitude, your brain responds with greater clarity and balance. This is called heart-brain coherence, and it is one of the most powerful ways to deepen awareness and access intuitive guidance.

Energetically, we also carry clutter, stuck emotions, outdated beliefs, and fear held in the chakras or the auric field. That's why energy practices like reiki, visualization, and intentional movement can shift the entire system. Dr. Beverly Rubik and Dr. William Tiller have shown in their research on the human biofield that our energetic system impacts our physical and emotional health (2002). This isn't just theory. It's measurable.

And as always, the science meets the spiritual.

Dr. Deepak Chopra's work in quantum healing explores how our consciousness, our thoughts, beliefs, and intentions, directly affect our physical body. His research, along with Dr. Bruce Lipton's work in epigenetics, shows that our emotions and environment can influence gene expression. In other words, how you breathe, move, and feel literally shapes your health and your future.

Because the more aware we become, the more present we become. And from that place, intuition flows.

In my own healing journey, these practices weren't rituals of perfection. They were lifelines—a walk, a breath, a dance. That's where awareness deepened. That's where I stopped identifying with my stress and started witnessing it. That's where I began to trust myself again. Because the more aware we become, the more present we become. And from that place, intuition flows.

Emotionally, presence invites us to get honest. To feel what we've pushed down. To pause long enough to notice. And spiritually, presence reconnects us to a deeper part of ourselves, which isn't ruled by fear or performance. It aligns us with our higher self.

I often guide clients to notice their breath and body in stillness, not to control anything, but to become aware of what's already there. Tightness in the chest? A clenching in the jaw? A flutter in the belly? These are messages. Presence is the first step to translating them. And when you notice without judgment, when you stay instead of flee, healing happens. Presence isn't passive. It's powerful. And it begins the moment you choose to return to yourself.

Reflection Questions:

What sensations, feelings, or messages come up when you pause and become still?

_____

_____

_____

_____

In what moments do you feel most connected to your body? What do those moments teach you?

_____

_____

_____

_____

How might you begin a practice of presence that includes both body and mind, even if just for a few minutes a day?

_____

_____

_____

_____

Action Step: Simple Presence-Building Exercises

You don't need hours of silence or a mountaintop retreat to be present. You just need a moment and a willingness to return to yourself. These simple practices are designed to help you build presence in a sustainable, intuitive way. They're not about perfection or doing it "right." They're about noticing what's real, right now, and learning to be with it, one breath at a time.

Choose one or two of the following to try this week. Try to add them into your normal routine, and when something doesn't connect as you hoped, go ahead and try something else. This is your journey.

1. Pause and Check-In

Take 60 seconds, at any point in your day, to pause and ask yourself:

What is happening in my body right now?
What am I feeling emotionally?
What do I need in this moment?

Place your hand over your heart or your belly. Take three slow, steady breaths. No fixing. Just noticing.

2. Sensory Grounding Walk

Go outside or walk slowly through your home. As you move, tune into your senses:

What are five things you can see?
Four things you can touch?
Three things you can hear?
Two things you can smell?
One thing you can taste?

This brings your attention out of the mind and into the body. It roots you in the present moment through your senses.

3. Body Awareness Meditation

Find a comfortable seat or lie down. Close your eyes or soften your gaze.

Take two to three deep breaths, breathing into your belly and completely releasing.

Gently scan your body from head to toe with your awareness.
Notice without judgment where you feel tension, ease, or sensation.
Breathe into any space that feels tight or heavy. Let it soften just a little.

Let your breath anchor you. Feel what's present and don't analyze. Know that your only job is to stay within yourself.

4. Intuitive Movement

Put on music that feels good and let your body move. There are no steps to follow. No right way to dance or stretch or sway. Just let your body speak. Ask, *What does my body want to do right now?* and then let it lead.

5. Create a "Presence Point"

Choose something you do every day, like brushing your teeth, making tea, or washing your hands, and use it as a presence ritual. Each time, slow down. Breathe. Feel your feet on the ground. Let that small moment become sacred.

Presence is a practice. And the more you choose it, the more your nervous system learns that *the now* is a safe place to be.

You've done something powerful by simply arriving in this moment. Presence isn't always comfortable, but it is always transformative. Every time you choose to pause instead of push, to feel instead of flee, you're rewriting the way your mind, body, and spirit respond to the world. Keep practicing, gently and consistently. These small moments of connection add up. They create space. They heal. And they bring you back to the truest part of you — the part that has always been worthy, even in stillness.

Chapter Summary: The Power of Presence—Mastering the Present Moment

Presence is not just about slowing down or learning to breathe more deeply. It's a courageous return to yourself. In this chapter, I shared the moments in my life when presence wasn't a luxury but a necessity. Through grief, silence, and reconnection, I began to understand that presence isn't something we have to earn. It's something we choose.

This chapter began not with meditation, but with memory. With grief. With a lake house and a little girl who slowly stopped feeling seen. It followed a thread through silence, resentment, reconciliation, and, finally, peace. I shared how presence came to me not through stillness first, but through survival. It was in the decision to leave the big house and find peace in a small mobile home filled with chaos and love. It was in the quiet reconnection with my father after the loss of my stepmother. It was in the final conversations we shared, the ones that healed old wounds not with perfect answers but with honest presence.

We explored how presence can be a healing force when we learn to let go of past stories and future fears. We looked at how the brain responds to mindfulness and how consistent presence changes the shape of your inner world, increasing clarity, reducing fear, and building resilience. Presence lowers cortisol, soothes the nervous system, and reconnects us to intuition. Spiritually, presence allows us to hear our own truth more clearly, to live from a place of trust rather than control. Through the lens of science, we looked at the work of Dr. Sara Lazar, Mihaly Csikszentmihalyi, and others who have shown that presence is not just a mindset. It's a full-body recalibration, a biological and energetic return to now.

This chapter also invited you to look at how past and future thinking can create anxiety and block your inner knowing. When you're living in memory or forecasting pain, you miss the voice of your own intuition. That voice, the one that knows, only lives in the present.

Through mindful movement, somatic awareness, heart coherence, and spiritual reconnection, presence becomes the doorway to transformation. Whether through journaling, dancing, walking barefoot in the yard, or simply leaving the dishes in the sink to laugh with the people I love, I found my way back. And you can, too.

The power of presence is not about perfection. It's about permission.

Presence is not something you have to perform. It's something you choose—not once, but moment by moment.

Whether it's through movement, breath, meditation, or stillness, your body holds the map back to the moment. You don't need a mountaintop. You just need the willingness to notice what's real and to honor it. The power of presence is not about perfection. It's about permission. To be here. To feel. To let go. And to come home to yourself again and again.

CHAPTER 9

Self-Love, Boundaries & Energy Protection

Personal Story: A Moment When I Had to Enforce a Boundary That Changed Everything

I was standing in the bathroom at work when it hit me. Not a thought, a sensation. A wave of dread rolled over me like a tide I hadn't seen coming, and yet, somehow, I had. My shoulders were hunched so tightly I could barely move. My jaw was clenched. My breath was shallow. I was grinding my teeth and didn't even realize it. I stood there, frozen, feeling the familiar tension. Then I heard his voice through the wall.

The owner of the company. My mentor. My tyrant. A man I had once looked up to, but now couldn't bear to be near. He was charismatic, powerful, and manipulative. He was brilliant and toxic. I had tolerated so much over the years: the inappropriate questions and forced conversations, the unwanted touches masked as friendly gestures, the psychological games, the endless demands. It was all suddenly crystal clear. I had been excusing behavior that was never okay. And I had been doing it for over 20 years.

Why was I still here?

I helped build that company. My brilliance, creativity, strategies, blood, sweat, and tears were in every corner of it. I had earned my seat at the table a hundred times over, and still, I felt like I had to keep proving it. My body had been trying to speak to me for years: the anaphylactic shock, the Lupus, the brain tumor, the autoimmune flares. I had ignored the whispers, then the

> *I had ignored the whispers, then the screams, of my own body until they nearly took me out.*

screams, of my own body until they nearly took me out. And still, I went back, just five weeks after major brain surgery, to the same office, the same system, the same stress. What did that say about how I valued myself?

For a long time, I thought it was just how things were. I was raised around someone just like him, someone who blurred the lines and used charm as a weapon. Inappropriate behavior didn't register as dangerous, it registered as normal and something women just had to navigate. I thought I was strong for enduring. I thought it was my job to adapt, survive, and keep producing.

But one day, I couldn't anymore.

Something inside me cracked open, and instead of fear pouring out, it was truth. I didn't want to stay in that cycle anymore. I began interviewing for other roles, high-level positions at respected companies that paid double what I was making. I impressed them. I got offers. And for the first time, I saw myself through someone else's eyes: powerful, brilliant, worthy.

There was a moment right before my brain tumor diagnosis when I started talking with another company. An opportunity that seemed like the perfect fit: global, innovative, aligned with my skillset. We were just starting the interview process when I received the news of my diagnosis. Everything came crashing down. I told them I understood if they needed to move on.

But they didn't. They waited.

They told me to take care of myself, and that when I was ready, the door would still be open. I couldn't believe the kindness and respect. That alone shifted something in me. Four weeks after brain surgery, with bruising still fading from my face and my body far from fully healed, I showed up for a full day of interviews. I covered what I could with makeup, but I didn't hide. I walked in with a quiet strength I hadn't fully owned before.

And what I walked into was something I'll never forget.

The atmosphere was light, not in the sense of being easy, but in the sense of being open. People smiled. They greeted each other by name. There was laughter in the hallways. During my tour, I watched teams actually enjoying their work, not just surviving it. There was collaboration, mutual respect, and a natural rhythm to how they supported one another. It was vibrant. It was warm. It felt safe.

In the conference room, I participated in Zoom meetings with owners from overseas. I answered technical questions and strategic challenges with ease and confidence. But it wasn't just my knowledge that shone, it was my presence. I wasn't trying to be impressive. I wasn't trying to prove myself. I was simply being who I had always been, just without the weight of fear sitting on my chest. That day, I remembered what it felt like to be in a space where people actually wanted to be. Where you didn't have to shrink to fit in. Where your brilliance was welcomed, not mined and manipulated. And it was stunning to realize how unfamiliar that feeling was.

I had spent over two decades in an environment where stress and dysfunction were normalized. Where boundaries were blurred, and exhaustion was glorified. Where I had learned to equate my worth with how much I could take on without complaint.

But there, in that new space, I didn't feel small. I felt seen. Not because I pushed through, but because I showed up as all of me: healing, whole, capable, worthy. It reminded me that I had choices, that the version of me who had spent years feeling like she had to endure was not the only version.

> *Not because I pushed through, but because I showed up as all of me: healing, whole, capable, worthy.*

So why didn't I take that job?

Even though this company reflected so much of what I deserved, the timing wasn't right. The commute was long. The hours were full-time. My healing still needed space. It wasn't the job that was wrong, it was the cost. And I had finally learned to stop making myself the sacrifice.

So I turned inward. What did I really want?

I wanted peace. I wanted space. I wanted to honor the body that had been trying to save my life for years. I wanted to live on my terms, not just exist within someone else's agenda.

I made a decision that changed everything. I requested a three-day work week, at a specific salary, in what was then my current role. I spoke with clarity, not apology. I didn't try to justify or explain why I deserved it. I simply asked. And when they said yes, something shifted in me forever.

I had reclaimed my power. Because I wasn't asking for permission. I was claiming what I was worth.

That experience, standing in a different culture, a healthier one, reminded me that it was never about the title or the paycheck. It was about the energy, the alignment—the way a place or person either makes you dim your light or helps you shine brighter.

And I chose to shine—on my terms.

It wasn't just about time or money. It was about choosing myself without guilt. It was about understanding that my worth wasn't tied to how much I could produce or how much I could endure. I wasn't there to burn myself out in order to be seen. I was there to thrive, to live fully, and to lead by example, starting with self-love.

You do not have to earn respect. You do not have to earn love. You are already worthy.

The version of me that said no wants you to know that you do not have to earn rest. You do not have to earn respect. You do not have to earn love. You are already worthy.

Boundaries are not walls. They are bridges back to yourself. And sometimes, the most loving thing you can do for your body, your spirit, and your future is to say yes to yourself.

Because when you say yes to yourself, the world begins to shift.

The Psychology of Self-Worth—Why We Struggle with Boundaries

The moment I stood in the bathroom, breath tight and body aching, was more than a sign of burnout. It was my nervous system telling me I wasn't safe. And for the first time, I truly heard it. I wasn't just exhausted. I was depleted. I had spent years tying my value to how much I could produce, how much I could carry, and how much I could endure. The work, the pressure, the inappropriate comments, the blurred boundaries—all of it had become part of my identity because somewhere deep down, I believed I had to earn my worth.

And that belief didn't start in the workplace. It started long before.

Our ability to set boundaries is deeply intertwined with how we see ourselves. If you were taught that love must be earned, or that worth is measured in output, it can feel unnatural, sometimes even wrong, to say no, to rest, or to want more. If you were raised in an environment where love felt conditional or where your needs were consistently secondary, you may have learned early that being "good" meant being quiet. That being lovable meant being useful. That rest had to be earned, and that value came from doing, not being.

Boundaries aren't a rejection of others. They're an invitation back to yourself, again and again.

This is where the psychology of self-worth intersects with boundaries. When you're taught that your worth is something external, you start overfunctioning. You say yes when your body screams no. You ignore the ache in your gut, the tightness in your chest, and the headaches that come every time you abandon yourself. And over time, that disconnect becomes normal.

Attachment theory and developmental psychology show us that early relationship patterns create the blueprint for how we engage with the world. If your childhood involved emotional caretaking, people-pleasing, or tiptoeing around someone else's moods, you likely internalized that setting a boundary risks rejection. That being visible means being vulnerable. That saying no might cost you love.

This conditioning often follows us into adulthood. It's what causes us to accept toxic work environments, overextend ourselves, or equate success with sacrifice. But boundaries aren't just about saying no, they're about choosing yourself. Boundaries aren't a rejection of others. They're an invitation back to yourself, again and again.

I didn't fully understand this until my body forced me to stop. I had pushed through illness, trauma, even brain surgery, believing my value came from how much I could endure. But in that moment, standing in the bathroom, hearing his voice through the wall, something in me snapped. It wasn't anger. It was truth. I finally realized that it wasn't strength, it was self-abandonment. And it had to stop.

Around that time, I had written down a quote from Glennon Doyle's *Untamed* and pinned it to the wall of my office studio. It read: "Disappoint as many people as you need to, to avoid disappointing yourself." It sat there for weeks before I could really understand it. But once I did, it became a mantra. A permission slip. A sacred boundary. That quote lived in my bones from the day I heard my mentor's voice through the wall. My body finally had enough.

Dr. Brené Brown's research on vulnerability and self-worth reminds us that "Daring to set boundaries is about having the courage to love ourselves even when we risk disappointing others" (2012). That quote on my wall? It echoed the same truth. It also helped me stop being the version of me who was endlessly available to others and completely absent to myself.

That wasn't defiance. That was healing.

The belief that says, *I have to do more to be worthy* is a cognitive distortion, a mental loop that gets reinforced over time until it becomes identity. And because of how the brain filters information through the RAS, it will actually scan for evidence that confirms this belief. So when you're praised for overdelivering or surviving stress, your brain says, *See? This is how I stay safe. This is how I stay loved.*

But you are not your patterns. You are not your output. And you are allowed to rewrite the narrative.

When you start questioning these beliefs and replacing them with truths, such as *My worth is not up for debate* and *I can be loved and still say no*, you begin to create new neural pathways that support peace, rather than performance. This is the mind's work: not just understanding boundaries intellectually, but embodying them through new decisions. According to Dr. Robert Sapolsky, chronic stress, especially in environments with blurred or violated boundaries, keeps cortisol levels high and damages the immune system, digestive system, and brain function. His research illustrates that the human body is not designed for prolonged stress. And yet, we normalize it in the name of success or "staying strong."

My own body kept the score through autoimmune conditions, inflammation and, eventually, a brain tumor. Now, I see those illnesses as truth-tellers—not punishment, but communication. My body wasn't betraying me. It was trying to protect me from what I had been taught to tolerate. Boundaries are not just functional. They are deeply spiritual. Saying no is a sacred act of remembering who you are. You are not here to shrink to fit someone else's expectations. You are not here to be defined by what you give away. You are not here to suffer in silence.

Your worth does not need proof. It needs honoring.

When I finally spoke my boundary, not just to the company, but to myself, something changed in my energy. I no longer felt like I was asking for too much. I was simply no longer available for less than I deserved. That was the moment self-worth stopped being an idea and became a lived experience.

Reflection Questions:

Where in your life have you been performing for love, rather than receiving it freely?

_____

_____

_____

_____

What old belief about your worth is no longer serving the person you truly are?

_____

_____

_____

_____

If your body had a voice right now, what would it say about the boundaries you've been avoiding?

_____

_____

_____

_____

The Science of Energy Protection — How Emotions, People, and Environments Affect You

We often talk about energy as if it's mystical, invisible, or just "vibes." But science shows us it's very real, measurable, impactful, and intimately tied to our health and clarity. Every room we walk into, every conversation we have, and every relationship we maintain has an energetic signature. And our nervous system feels it whether we're conscious of it or not.

I didn't always understand this. For years, I lived in environments that drained me, worked with people who didn't respect boundaries, and pushed myself to keep going when my body was crying for rest. I stayed because it was what I knew. But I didn't realize the cost until my body made it impossible to ignore. I wasn't just physically exhausted. I was energetically depleted.

Protecting your energy doesn't require isolation or defensiveness; it requires awareness.

When I began interviewing with other companies after my brain surgery, the difference was immediate. The moment I stepped through the doors, I felt lightness, respect, and collaboration. It wasn't about whether the work was easy or hard. It was about the energy. The way people greeted one another. The smiles that weren't forced. The calm presence in the room. No tension. No walking on eggshells. No invisible weight in the air. For the first time in years, my nervous system exhaled.

Science confirms this energetic sensitivity. According to research by Dr. Beverly Rubik and Dr. William Tiller, the human biofield, our body's electromagnetic field, responds to emotional and environmental input. That means your energy field can become disrupted by chronic stress, toxic conversations, even fluorescent lighting or background tension. These disruptions often show up physically, before we even notice them emotionally, through fatigue, headaches, poor digestion, or trouble sleeping.

The HeartMath Institute adds to this understanding by showing that the heart sends more electrical signals to the brain than the brain sends to the heart. This means your emotional state isn't just a feeling, it becomes a cognitive lens. When your energy is off, your thoughts become foggy, reactive, and scattered. When your energy is grounded, your thoughts become clear, intuitive, and expansive.

We've all had the experience of walking into a room and instantly feeling on edge. Or getting off a phone call and feeling inexplicably drained. Your body is tracking more than just words. It's reading the field. Protecting your energy doesn't require isolation or defensiveness; it requires awareness. It's recognizing the signals early—the tension in your gut, the dull ache behind your eyes, the urge to retreat or shut down—and making choices that bring you back to center. Because you can't create a fulfilling, soul-aligned life from a place of depletion.

Energy drains often begin with small leaks—a yes that should've been a no, a conversation that went too long, a habit that no longer feels good. Left unaddressed, they accumulate and cloud your clarity. Your body will always signal misalignment—for example, through chronic fatigue, digestive issues, shallow breathing, or a feeling of heaviness. These symptoms are not random, they are messengers from your nervous system. Your energy is sacred. When it's scattered or absorbed by others' emotions, your intuition dims. But when you protect it, you become a clearer channel for your purpose, your creativity, and your inner guidance.

Energetic boundaries are not about shutting people out. They are about tuning into yourself first, so you know what's yours, what isn't, and what you're no longer available for. You are not responsible for carrying what drains you. You are responsible for choosing what sustains you. And that choice can change everything.

Reflection Questions:

What environments, conversations, or people leave you feeling drained, even if nothing "bad" is said or done?

_____

_____

_____

_____

How does your body let you know when your energy is off? What physical or emotional signs tend to show up?

_____

_____

_____

_____

What does energetic safety feel like to you, and how can you begin protecting that feeling more intentionally?

_____

_____

_____

_____

How to Prioritize Yourself Without Guilt and Set and Honor Healthy Boundaries That Fuel Your Energy

One of the most radical things you can do for your healing and your alignment is put yourself first. Without apology. Without guilt. Without explanation.

For many of us, that feels impossible. Maybe even wrong. Especially if your identity has been shaped by being the helper, the fixer, and the one who holds it all together. Guilt rises like a reflex, not because you're doing something wrong, but because you're doing something different.

That's exactly what I felt when I finally decided to ask for a three-day workweek. After all those years of over-performing, overextending, and over-functioning, a part of me still wondered: *Is this allowed? Will I lose respect? Will I still be seen as valuable if I'm not burning out to prove it?* But my body was done. My spirit was louder than my fear. And after seeing how I showed up for other

I realized I had been waiting for permission I didn't need.

companies—respected, valued, whole—I knew I couldn't keep shrinking to survive. I didn't want more money or another title. I wanted alignment.

So I asked for it: a schedule that supported my health, a salary that honored my contributions, a life that made space for recovery, creativity, and joy. And when they said yes, something shifted in me forever. I realized I had been waiting for permission I didn't need.

Neuroscience shows us that the brain doesn't change just by thinking new thoughts; it rewires through repetition and action. When you start enforcing boundaries, your nervous system may initially sound the alarm. That's because your brain associates "no" with the risk of disapproval, conflict, or rejection. But this is where neuroplasticity becomes your ally. Each time you choose a small act of self-honoring—leaving work on time, saying no to a draining commitment, taking rest when your body asks—you're building new neural pathways that say *peace is safe, rest is productive, I am enough.*

You don't have to start with big changes. You start by listening to yourself and responding with love instead of fear. Your body is the most accurate compass you have. When something feels like expansion, it's spacious, energizing, and open. Your body will tell you. When something feels like depletion, it's constriction, exhaustion, and dread. Your body will tell you that, too. Ayurvedic teachings remind us that the body thrives on rhythm, on cycles of rest and activity, and honoring its unique constitution and capacity. When you override those needs in the name of productivity or people-pleasing, your health pays the price.

Tracking your energy daily and honestly is a way of building self-trust. It's not selfish. It's strategic. Because when you protect your energy, you expand your capacity to give in ways that are sustainable and joyful. Spiritually, boundaries are sacred. They say, *I will no longer abandon myself to belong.* They are permission slips to be whole, to let your soul breathe, and to create room for your purpose to unfold.

You can be kind and still say no. You can be compassionate and still walk away. You can be generous and still choose rest. The more you choose yourself, the more others learn how to meet you at that level.

This isn't about building walls. It's about building trust, especially with yourself, first.

You don't just say no to that old system. You say yes to healing. To creativity. To the future version of you who gets to live with ease. And that is what real power looks like. Not sacrifice, but sovereignty.

Reflection Questions:

What old belief still whispers that you're only valuable when you're overextending?

_____

_____

_____

_____

How does your body feel when you honor your limits? What does that tell you?

_____

_____

_____

_____

If guilt didn't get a vote, what boundary would you set this week?

_____

_____

_____

_____

The Truth About Boundaries: They Are Yours to Hold

There's a truth I come back to again and again in my own healing, in my coaching, and in the real-life challenges my clients face: Most people expect others to honor their boundaries, but forget that boundaries are only as strong as the person willing to uphold them.

Boundaries are not about what others do. They are about what *you choose*, how you respond, what you allow and hold sacred. This is one of the biggest shifts we make in the healing journey: from blaming others for crossing our boundaries to asking ourselves why we didn't uphold them.

Boundaries are not about what others do. They are about what you choose, how you respond, what you allow and hold sacred.

And this is not about guilt, it's about grace. We don't know what we haven't been taught. Most of us were conditioned to believe that love, approval, and peace depended on our ability to over-give, stay quiet, or keep the harmony at our own expense. It's no wonder so many of us struggle to say no, or worse, say it and then feel ashamed for doing so. But science helps us understand why this struggle is so deeply ingrained.

As we explored earlier, the nervous system is shaped by experience. Dr. Stephen Porges's Polyvagal Theory explains how environments that felt unsafe or unpredictable trained our bodies to associate "no" with threat, rejection, punishment, or abandonment. In those moments, it may not be a conscious decision to abandon our boundaries but a stress response, rooted in survival. Dr. Brené Brown puts it beautifully: "Daring to set boundaries is about having the courage to love ourselves even when we risk disappointing others."

Your brain, especially the RAS, filters the world based on what you believe about your worth. If you believe your value lies in what you do for others, you'll notice every opportunity to overextend. You'll feel pulled to overfunction, even when your body says no.

This is why boundary work must include the mind, body, and spirit. You are rewiring beliefs that say your worth is earned. As you set and hold boundaries, new neural pathways form. Over time, your brain learns that rest, saying no, and prioritizing yourself are safe. Your body is your greatest teacher. It will whisper to you before it screams. If a situation causes tension in your jaw, tightness in your chest, or a spike of adrenaline, listen. As Dr.

Sapolsky's work shows, unrelenting stress leads to inflammation, burnout, and autoimmune illness. Boundaries are not just emotional, they're physiological protection.

Spiritually, holding a boundary is an act of reverence. It says, *I trust myself. I honor my inner voice. I will not abandon myself to make others comfortable.* This is not selfish. It's sacred. When you protect your energy, you make space for peace, creativity, and soul alignment.

But remember, it's not about perfection.

There will be times when you give in, and that's okay. There will be moments when you say yes even though your body whispers no. That doesn't mean you failed. It means you're learning. You're experimenting. You're practicing. Boundaries aren't rigid lines. They are living conversations with yourself. And each time you check in and choose based on *your truth*— not fear, not obligation, not guilt—you build self-trust.

You are allowed to change your mind. You are allowed to hold a boundary one day and shift it the next. What matters is that you keep coming back to yourself. That you listen. That you stay curious.

Before you step into the action step, take a moment to revisit the reflection questions in this chapter. What patterns did you recognize? What moments in your life asked you to shrink, and what would it feel like to expand instead?

Because the most powerful boundaries don't scream. They don't punish.

They whisper, *I matter. And I choose myself now.*

Action Step: Define Three Non-Negotiables for Self-Care

Self-care isn't selfish. It's structure. It's sustainability. It's how you protect your energy, reclaim your time, and honor the truth of what you need to feel safe, whole, and well in order to thrive.

When you define your non-negotiables, you're not just creating a routine, you're creating a boundary. One that says, *I matter. My body matters. My joy matters. My health matters. My peace matters.*

This is how you begin to live in alignment, not all at once, but one clear choice at a time.

Step 1: Revisit What Resonated Most

Go back to the reflection questions in this chapter. Take a deep breath. Let yourself re-read what you wrote, or journal quietly through the questions you skipped.

What stands out now?

_____

_____

_____

_____

What did my body need that I didn't honor?

_____

_____

_____

_____

Where have I been shrinking, overextending, or abandoning myself?

_____

_____

_____

_____

What would shift if I believed peace and rest were not rewards, but rights?

_____

_____

_____

_____

Let your answers guide you. You're not setting boundaries from fear or defense; you're setting them from truth, from love, and from a desire to stop performing and start living.

Step 2: Define Three Non-Negotiables

Choose three boundaries, practices, or commitments that will support your nervous system, your energy, and your soul this month. These should feel nourishing, supportive, and doable. They can be small. They just need to be real.

Examples:

- I do not check my email before 9 a.m.

- I pause before saying yes, even to "small" requests.

- I move my body in a way that feels good, three times per week.

- I say no to anything that creates resentment in my body.

- I protect one evening a week for stillness, creativity, or joy.

- I no longer justify my boundaries. I hold them with softness and strength.

Write down your three non-negotiables. Let them be clear. Let them reflect who you are now, not who you used to be, or who someone else expects you to be.

_____

_____

_____

_____

Step 3: Anchor Them In

Boundaries are not set-and-forget. They are living choices. To support them, choose one or more anchoring rituals:

- Create a short mantra like: *Peace is my priority. I choose myself.*

- Set a daily phone reminder with your favorite boundary-based mantra.

- Write your three on a sticky note for your mirror, fridge or journal.

- Share one with a trusted friend, partner, or coach.

- Use a treasured quote that reminds you of your boundary.

I keep the one from Glennon Doyle on my wall:

"Disappoint as many people as you need to, to avoid disappointing yourself."

These are not rules. These are reflections of your *self-worth in motion.* They are not here to confine you, they're here to protect your light. These are anchors, a foundation to come back to when life gets loud.

Remember: Your boundaries will grow with you. They are not fixed rules, but living reflections of your truth. Your non-negotiables may shift as your needs change, and that is not a failure. It is a sign that you are listening. Returning to them, especially in moments of discomfort, is how you build trust with yourself—not because you always get it right, but because you are willing to stay present with your own growth. That is what self-love really looks like.

This is how you begin to move from burnout into balance, from performing who you think you should be to embodying who you actually are. You do not need permission to take up space. You do not need to be exhausted to deserve rest. You are allowed to change.

Let your non-negotiables be your compass—not just a checklist, but a gentle guide back to what matters most. Let them remind you that peace is not something you have to earn. It is something you are allowed to choose.

Summary: Returning to Yourself Through Boundaries, Energy, and Self-Love

There was a time when I believed that boundaries were walls. That they would push people away or make me seem difficult. I was the one who said yes to everything. Who overdelivered. Who adapted to chaos and called it strength. And for a long time, I didn't question that rhythm, even when it was breaking me.

But the truth is, the body always tells the truth. And mine had been whispering for years before it screamed. The autoimmune flares, the anxiety, the brain tumor—none of it came out of nowhere. It was the result of years of self-abandonment, of living in environments where my worth was measured by how much I could endure. It wasn't until everything came to a breaking point that I finally understood—I wasn't weak for needing space. I was wise for finally honoring it.

The moment I drew that first real boundary, everything shifted. It wasn't just about refusing toxic behavior or stepping back from work that depleted me. It was about reclaiming a part of myself I had long abandoned. I realized I wasn't there to survive anymore. I was ready to heal. I was ready to choose peace over performance, presence over people-pleasing. That boundary wasn't a rejection of others, it was a return to myself.

Boundaries are not selfish. They are self-honoring. They are how we say, "I matter," not just in words, but in how we choose to live, work, and heal. They're not about shutting people out, they're about creating space for the parts of you that have been silenced. What I've learned, through my own healing and in supporting others, is that boundaries are not something we set once. They're something we learn to live, day by day, moment by moment. They are not walls. They are clarity. And they're how we honor the connection between our mind, our body, and our spirit.

Your nervous system cannot relax in environments that constantly pull you into fear or depletion. Your body cannot heal if you are constantly overriding its needs. And your soul cannot express its truth if you are always shrinking to meet someone else's expectations. Boundaries change that. Energy protection is not just spiritual, it is scientific, practical, and essential. Your body and nervous system register everything, even the things you convince yourself to tolerate. When you ignore your energy, you exhaust your capacity to create, connect, and thrive. But when you begin to notice what drains you and honor what restores you, everything shifts.

Worth is not earned through suffering. You are worthy now. Not when you've achieved enough. Not when everyone else is happy. Not when you've proven how strong you are. Now. In your imperfection. In your truth. And most of all, saying no to what drains you is how you say yes to what heals you. It's how you choose your future over your past. Your peace over your performance. Your alignment over approval.

> *You are worthy now. Not when you've achieved enough. Not when everyone else is happy. Not when you've proven how strong you are. Now.*

So if you've been afraid to draw that line, to speak your truth, to choose yourself, start small. Let this chapter be your invitation to come back to what matters most: **you**.

Because the moment you stop abandoning yourself is the moment you begin to come home.

CHAPTER 10

Building Your Mission Me 2.0 Blueprint

Personal Story: A Lesson on Sustaining Transformation Beyond a Single Breakthrough

There's a myth in the personal growth world that healing is a finish line. That once you've had your breakthrough, everything falls into place. I never believed transformation was a one-time event. From the moment I started this work, I understood I was beginning a lifelong process. Healing, for me, has always been a layered journey, a process of peeling back, discovering, questioning, and honoring the responsibility I hold for my own evolution. As a yoga instructor once said, "Perhaps you are not responsible for the wounds, but you are responsible for your healing." That stayed with me. I took it to heart.

Every chapter of this book has held a lesson, not just from my past, but from my present. I'm still learning. I'm still noticing.

I notice it when I'm overwhelmed by clutter and suddenly feel that old compulsion rise, the one that says, *You can't rest until everything is perfect.* I notice it when I go to clean and spend hours on one room, not because it needs to be that clean, but because I've slipped into a trance of control. That's why I pay someone to help me clean every two weeks. Not because I'm incapable, but because I know my patterns. I know how quickly I can lose time, joy, and peace to perfectionism masked as productivity. That awareness is part of my healing.

> I know how quickly I can lose time, joy, and peace to perfectionism masked as productivity.

The deeper I went, the more I uncovered patterns that had lived so quietly in the background, I didn't even question them until they began to feel out of place. One of those patterns was around gift-giving and receiving.

For many years, holidays and birthdays felt like competitions. Who gave the best gift? Who spent the most? Our kids were showered with so many presents they couldn't possibly remember them all. I used to say it was because they had three sets of grandparents, and that was true, but it was more than that. It was about status, performance, and proving something. I got swept into it. I thought that was what love looked like. I didn't realize how much pressure I was carrying.

Looking back, it made sense. I had been the only grandchild on my father's side for years. I was spoiled with gifts. Maybe they were trying to make up for the chaos at home. Maybe that was their way of saying, "We see you. You matter." As I got older, I began to see how deeply my dad's love language was rooted in giving. Jewelry, electronics, wish lists fulfilled—it was always about more. Generosity, in his world, was how you showed value. But sometimes, it felt like it was more about his value than mine. A way to say, "Look what I can do. Look what I gave."

As I began to do the deeper emotional work, gift-giving started to feel transactional. It didn't feel as meaningful anymore. It felt performative—how the pressure to impress or perform for love once ruled our holidays, how I used to equate love with more. More presents, more effort, more proving. Until I started asking why. Until I started giving differently. Choosing connection over cost. Meaning over materials. So I shifted. I started making gifts by hand or choosing experiences instead, like tickets to a show together, a night out—something shared. I wanted presence, not performance. Connection, not currency.

I felt it when I was standing in the bathroom at work, exhausted and broken, hearing the voice of a man who had mentored and manipulated me. The clarity that rose in that moment wasn't just about him; it was about every time I'd stayed silent, over-functioned, or allowed my boundaries to be eroded in the name of being "nice" or "needed." That moment changed everything. But it didn't end there.

Each of these moments was a thread. And together, they're the fabric of a life rebuilt.

Transformation came again when I turned down a job offer from a company that felt aligned because my body wasn't ready. Because healing mattered more than achievement. Because I finally believed I didn't need to prove anything. Each of these moments was a thread. And together, they're the fabric of a life rebuilt.

That awareness continues to grow. Just when I think I've healed a pattern, another version of it shows up. I catch myself in old habits: overcompensating, overgiving, overfunctioning. But now I notice. I breathe. I ask questions. I pause.

Healing is not a destination. It's how I wake up each day and ask: *Where am I betraying myself to stay comfortable? What part of me needs to be seen, loved, or released? What's mine to carry today, and what's not?*

These days, I've pulled way back. The holidays are quieter and more intentional. I've traded piles of things for a few meaningful gifts and the presence of the people I love. It feels lighter. Real.

This journey has taught me that transformation is sustained not through force, but through attention. Through honoring my patterns without judgment. Through catching myself when the Windsock Guy reappears in my nervous system. When I'm flailing in all directions, trying to keep everyone else comfortable and forgetting myself in the process.

It's in these moments I remember: I've been here before. When I left the big house by the lake at 16 for a trailer full of love and chaos, it wasn't just a move, but a decision to choose peace over performance. When I paused in the kitchen instead of diving into the dishes, I chose presence over programming. When I said no to the job that looked perfect on paper but asked too much of my healing body, I chose alignment over achievement. And when I stood in the bathroom, exhausted by years of manipulation and noise, and finally said, "No more," I chose truth over tolerance.

Each of those moments, from the quiet healing in my yoga practice to the deep grief that carved space for reconnection, was a page in my blueprint. Not one of them was the final breakthrough. They were invitations. Reminders. Markers along the path.

And now, I see that's what this work is. Not a before-and-after story. A series of returns. To yourself. To your body. To your breath. To what matters. That's what this chapter is really about—not the breakthrough itself, but the commitment to continue. To notice the patterns that sneak back in. To meet them with compassion. To choose again. Because evolution doesn't happen once. It happens every time you decide to live in alignment with the person you're becoming. To presence. To simplicity. To the practices that help you feel grounded, clear, and connected. Because transformation isn't about arriving. It's about remembering. Again and again.

So when the old patterns knock, when perfectionism sneaks in or people-pleasing raises its voice or the Windsock flutters for someone else's storm, I pause. I ask. I feel. I come back. Not to who I used to be. But to who I'm becoming.

It's not about being perfect. It's about being in a relationship with yourself. About learning to listen deeper and live with more awareness, so that you don't lose yourself in the noise of the world.

> *It's not about being perfect. It's about being in a relationship with yourself.*

This is what it means to build a life, not around your past or your pain, but around your peace.

Creating a Long-Term Strategy for Continued Transformation

Transformation doesn't end when the breakthrough happens. That's when the real work begins. The truth is, no one climbs a mountain and stays at the summit forever. You take in the view, feel the power of how far you've come, and then... you keep moving. You build your life from that perspective, not just toward it. Transformation doesn't live in grand declarations. It lives in the follow-through. In the small, daily choices you make to return to yourself, especially when life pulls you off track. Transformation doesn't end with the "aha" moment. It begins there. Sustainable change is built in the small, consistent choices that follow the breakthrough, in the integration.

It's easy to feel inspired in the middle of a breakthrough. But what sustains transformation is structure. Not rigidity, but rhythm. Something that feels like *you*. Something that fits into your real life, not an idealized version of who you think you should be. In order to sustain change, you need a rhythm, not a rigid plan. Life is unpredictable. Your needs will shift. Your energy will fluctuate. What worked for you in one season might feel misaligned in the next. That's not failure—it's evolution.

Your nervous system craves familiarity. Change feels risky, even when it's positive. That's why intentional habits matter. When you repeat something new with presence, it stops being "new," and becomes safe. This is the foundation of neuroplasticity. You're literally rewiring your brain toward ease and empowerment. Your body remembers what feels good.

What feels safe. What feels aligned. That's why rituals like morning grounding, movement, or hydration aren't "extras." They are the scaffolding that holds your transformation in place. Ayurveda and integrative healing both affirm that rhythm creates resilience. Your soul thrives on alignment. It knows when you're honoring your truth and when you're abandoning yourself. Long-term transformation requires sacred pause, space to listen inward, reflect, and realign. That's where your truth lives.

From a neuroscience standpoint, research on neuroplasticity reminds us that change happens through repeated, intentional action. Neuroscience tells us that lasting transformation requires repetition. According to research by Dr. Donald Hebb, "neurons that fire together, wire together" (1949). This is the foundation of neuroplasticity: your brain rewires itself based on your focus, habits, and environment. So when you choose a new thought, a new boundary, and a new way of being, you begin building a new neural pathway. New neural pathways are created not in the intensity of one decision, but in the consistency of many. Every time you choose rest over reactivity, boundaries over burnout, or alignment over approval, you're carving a new path in your brain and in your life. It's not instant. But it's real.

Your long-term strategy starts by asking better questions:

- What do I want to feel like in this next season?
- What are the practices that anchor me when life gets loud?
- Where do I need structure, and where do I need softness?

In Ayurveda and holistic psychology, this is echoed through daily rituals like dinacharya that keep you in rhythm with your truest self. Transformation isn't always loud or dramatic. It's often quiet, intentional, and rhythmic, like returning to the breath.

Your blueprint might include:

- Weekly check-ins with yourself or your coach.

- A monthly ritual to reassess what's working, what's not, and what you want to do differently.

- A list of your "anchors," or practices, people, or places that keep you grounded.

- A commitment to presence, not perfection.

You don't need a perfect system. You need a living one. One that grows with you. One that lets you evolve without abandoning your needs. Spiritually, this becomes a sacred agreement with yourself. A blueprint not built on pressure, but on presence.

This strategy isn't about doing more. It's about living more honestly, creating space to check in with your energy, review your non-negotiables, and adjust as needed. This is your framework for transformation: flexible, intuitive, and aligned.

Soul meets structure when you create a blueprint that works with your nervous system. You can ask:

- What tools help me return to presence?
- What rhythms support my clarity?
- How do I build support around my healing?

This is your blueprint. One that honors your mind, supports your body, and reflects your spirit. Not anyone else's.

Reflection Questions:

What do I want to feel in this next season of my life, and what rhythms or rituals will help me return to that feeling when life pulls me off track?

_____

_____

_____

_____

What practices, people, or places consistently help me feel safe, grounded, and aligned with my truth?

_____

_____

_____

_____

How can I create a living blueprint for my transformation, one that supports my nervous system, honors my soul, and evolves with me?

_____

_____

_____

_____

How to Maintain Motivation, Alignment, and Consistency

You don't stay aligned by force. You stay aligned by remembering why you started. The key to sustainable change isn't willpower, it's alignment. When you feel off track, the answer isn't to push harder. It's to come back into alignment. We often think motivation is the spark that keeps us going, but motivation fades. Alignment is what sustains.

When your actions are rooted in your values, when they match your truth, consistency becomes less about discipline and more about devotion. In my journey, there were days I lost momentum. Days I didn't feel inspired, but when I leaned into rhythm. Into remembering. Into the small rituals that brought me back.

Motivation fades when your *why* is unclear. Revisit it often. Write it down. Speak it aloud. Let it evolve. Keep it personal, not performative. When your goals are connected to your core values, consistency becomes self-honoring, not self-punishing. Consistency doesn't mean doing the same thing every day. It means doing what your body needs most in that moment. Some days, that's movement. Other days, rest. Learn to ask, "What would feel supportive right now?" and trust the answer. This is embodiment. Alignment requires presence. When you're out of sync, your energy will tell you. You'll feel disconnected, resentful, or overwhelmed. These are not failures—they're signals. Use them as invitations to return to what matters.

When your actions are rooted in your values, when they match your truth, consistency becomes less about discipline and more about devotion.

The Self-Determination Theory in psychology tells us that sustainable motivation stems from autonomy, competence, and connection (Deci & Ryan, 1985). In other words, sustained motivation is driven by three core psychological needs:

- Autonomy: feeling in charge of your own path. (You need to feel that you are making empowered choices.)

- Competence: believing you can create change. (You need to feel capable of growth.)

- Relatedness: feeling connected to something greater than yourself. (You need to feel connected to something greater, such as a purpose, a community, or a calling.)

This is why your transformation must be self-led, self-honoring, and connected to your deeper "why." Spiritually, alignment is about resonance. When your outer life reflects your inner truth, motivation becomes magnetic.

You're not pushing, you're being pulled. Your consistency isn't about perfection. It's about devotion. A devotion to peace. A devotion to showing up for yourself even on the hard days. Especially on the hard days.

What would consistency look like if it felt like support instead of pressure? This is why cookie-cutter routines fail. Because when we follow someone else's path instead of listening to our own, motivation dies out. True consistency is born when the actions you take are in harmony with the person you're becoming. It's your intuition calling you forward. The quiet knowing that says, *Keep going. This matters.*

That's why we revisit our intentions. We don't just ask, "What do I need to do?" We ask, "Who am I becoming? What choices support that?" And when your mind wanders or your energy dips, you come back to your breath, to your *why*, and to your blueprint. That's the practice.

Tools like habit stacking, body-based anchoring, and ritualizing joy help integrate new habits in a way that feels nourishing, not punishing.

Ask yourself:
- Where does motivation feel forced?
- Where does it feel natural?

Tip: Choose sustainable over dramatic. Choose supportive over impressive. Choose your own rhythm over someone else's routine.

Reflection Questions:

What signals does my body give me when I'm out of alignment, and what helps me gently return to center without judgment?

_____

_____

_____

_____

What does devotion look like for me right now—not perfection, but a quiet, steady commitment to my growth?

_____

_____

_____

_____

Where in my life am I following someone else's rhythm or routine, and what would shift if I trusted my own?

_____

_____

_____

_____

Recognizing Self-Sabotage Patterns and How to Course-Correct and Maintain Momentum

Self-sabotage isn't weakness—it's protection. We all self-sabotage. Not because we're lazy or broken, but because our brains are wired for safety. And growth, even beautiful growth, can feel threatening to the part of you that was trained to survive, not thrive. Every path of growth comes with resistance. Not because you're broken, but because you're growing. Self-sabotage isn't a flaw in your character. It's a protective mechanism of your nervous system, rooted in past experiences.

Self-sabotage sounds like:

- "I'll start again Monday."
- "This doesn't feel like it's working."
- "Who am I to change?"
- "Maybe I was doing better before."

> *Self-sabotage isn't a flaw in your character. It's a protective mechanism of your nervous system, rooted in past experiences.*

These are not truths. They are protection strategies.

Your brain will try to bring you back to what's familiar. That's not failure, that's a chance to notice. Patterns repeat until they are witnessed. Then, they can be rewired. Self-sabotage often shows up as fatigue, distraction, or disconnection. When you suddenly want to scroll instead of journal, nap instead of move, or isolate instead of reach out, pause. Ask, "What am I avoiding? What needs care right now?" Your spirit doesn't sabotage. It waits. It nudges. It reminds you of who you are. When you feel off course, come back to your truth. You are not starting over. You are resuming, with more awareness than before.

In internal family systems, sabotage is often a protector part, a younger or wounded aspect of you, trying to keep you safe in old ways. The version of you that says, *This won't last*, or *Who do you think you are?* is the same version that once learned safety through staying small.

But now, you know better. You know how to listen with compassion, not criticism. You've seen the sabotage before—in the overthinking, the scrolling, the last-minute canceling, the resentment that creeps in when you abandon your boundaries.

Try this course-correction process:

- Notice without shame. "Something feels off."
- Pause before reacting. "This is my perfectionism," or "This is fear speaking."

- Ask, "What do I need right now?" or "What's the most loving next step?"
- Return gently. Even a 1% shift is progress.

This is why self-compassion is the medicine. When you notice yourself slipping into old patterns, instead of punishment, offer pause, reflection, curiosity, and compassion. This is how you become consistent: by being kind, not controlling. No one wants to be controlled, even by themselves. Be kind to yourself.

Dr. Bruce Lipton's work in epigenetics and subconscious reprogramming shows that up to 95% of our behaviors are driven by unconscious patterns, which means your sabotage isn't about willpower, it's about wiring. And wiring can be changed. It shows us that our environments, thoughts, and emotions literally influence gene expression. If your default is fear or depletion, your cells respond. But when you shift toward intention, regulation, and rest, your biology responds, too. That's why the first step is compassion. When you notice yourself procrastinating, overcommitting, or numbing out, ask:

- What am I protecting myself from?
- What fear is underneath this behavior?
- What part of me needs safety, not shame?

The moments when you're pulled in every direction, trying to meet everyone's expectations, are cues. The flailing is a symptom. The root is often fear: fear of being seen, fear of not being enough, fear of change. Change your inner narrative. You control you, and only you.

When you notice the pattern, you reclaim your power. You step out of the loop and back into intention. Course correction isn't dramatic, it's gentle. It's the breath you take before you say yes out of guilt. The pause you insert before you scroll. The moment you re-anchor to your *why* and choose again. Awareness in its full light.

Spiritually, this is where grace meets growth. There is no perfect path, just the path you keep returning to, one honest step at a time. I have faith in you. If I can do it, you can, too. I am happier, healthier, and more fulfilled every day, and I keep grace and compassion at the ready for those moments when I know I need them.

Reflection Questions:

When I notice myself slipping into distraction, overthinking, or avoidance, what might I actually need in that moment?

_____

_____

_____

_____

What protective story from my past am I still carrying? How can I begin to meet it with compassion instead of control?

_____

_____

_____

_____

What would it look like to return to myself gently, without shame, when I fall into old patterns?

_____

_____

_____

_____

Action Step: Create Your Personalized Blueprint for Sustainable Transformation

Insight without integration won't create the change you seek. Transformation isn't just something you _understand_, it's something you _live_. And living it requires more than motivation. It requires mindful structure, nervous system safety, and a deeper connection to what feels true for you.

This blueprint is not about perfection or pressure. It's about creating a flexible, intentional rhythm that supports your mind, nurtures your body, and honors your inner truth. It's rooted in the science of sustainable behavior change and built through mindful action, one step at a time.

Let's begin.

Step 1: Clarify Your _Why_

Your nervous system stays engaged when your actions are connected to meaning. Write down your _why_, the reason behind your desire for change.

What do you want to feel more of? What values are you choosing to live by right now?

_____

_____

_____

_____

Step 2: Set One to Three Foundational Daily Anchors

Choose simple, repeatable habits that support your well-being, physically, mentally, and emotionally. These can shift as your needs shift.

Examples:

- Morning breath awareness
- Midday screen-free pause
- Evening walk or stretch

Start with small actions that feel calming, not overwhelming. Your brain wires through repetition, not intensity.

_____

_____

_____

_____

Step 3: Create a Weekly Self-Check-In

Consistency thrives when we pause and reflect. Choose one moment each week to ask:

- What's working?
- What's draining me?
- What's one small shift I want to make?

This builds cognitive awareness and keeps your nervous system engaged in active, supported change.

_____

_____

_____

_____

Step 4: Identify Your Support System

List three sources of support: people, places, or practices. Support doesn't mean dependence. It means resourcing yourself wisely.

Who reminds you of your truth when you forget?

_____

_____

_____

_____

What spaces help you reset?

_____

_____

_____

_____

What tools bring clarity or calm?

_____

_____

_____

_____

Step 5: Recognize & Reframe Your Sabotage Patterns

When resistance shows up, it's not failure, it's feedback. List one to three common patterns, such as procrastination, overthinking, and checking out. Next to each, write one regulating practice or reframing thought that helps you move through it. *Example: When I start to freeze or scroll, I'll take three grounding breaths and ask: "What am I really needing right now?"*

_____

_____

_____

_____

Step 6: Choose One to Three Monthly Intentions

Intentions guide action with awareness. Set one to three clear, supportive intentions for the next 30 days. Keep them realistic and rooted in presence, such as:

- "I will honor my energy without guilt."
- "I will speak kindly to myself, even when I slip."
- "I will move my body for clarity, not punishment."

_____

_____

_____

_____

Step 7: Ritualize the Commitment

This can be as simple as creating a mantra or code, taking three deep breaths, or placing your hand over your heart. Mark the moment. Let your body feel the shift.

This is a declaration of presence—not to the world, but to yourself.

This is not a fixed formula. This is a living agreement between you and the version of yourself you are becoming. Neuroscience reminds us that small, intentional steps repeated with awareness can literally rewire the brain. Your body will remember what feels safe, supportive, and aligned. And when life pulls you off course, because it will, you'll know how to return. Not with shame, but with presence.

Your blueprint is yours alone. Let it evolve with you.

Summary: The Practice of Becoming

There was a time when I believed transformation would feel like a moment. Like some grand turning point where everything clicked into place and stayed there. But it didn't happen like that. My healing has unfolded in layers, in patterns I barely noticed until they felt out of place, and in questions I hadn't thought to ask until the moment they mattered most. Some quiet, some loud, all asking me to choose again.

> These moments weren't failures. They were invitations. And each time I noticed, I was offered a choice: return to the old pattern or return to myself.

I began to notice the patterns I used to miss, the ways old habits crept in. How I could lose hours deep cleaning one room, not because it needed to be done, but because I was chasing control. I noticed the pressure I used to feel around holidays and gifts, as if love had to be proven through effort or price. These moments weren't failures. They were invitations. And each time I noticed, I was offered a choice: return to the old pattern or return to myself. They were quiet reminders to pause, to breathe, and to return to what matters.

This chapter wasn't just about the insight. It was about what happens after. It was about how you keep going when the energy fades, when the excitement wears off, and when old beliefs try to pull you back into who you used to be.

You explored what it takes to sustain transformation in a way that feels nourishing, not exhausting. You learned that long-term change is not built on willpower alone. It's supported by alignment. Neuroscience reminds us that every time you make an intentional choice, you are wiring your brain toward ease and clarity. Small steps, repeated with presence, lead to lasting change. That's the power of neuroplasticity.

You also looked at motivation through a different lens. When your actions reflect your values, consistency stops being a chore and becomes a form of self-respect. You're not pushing yourself toward some imagined version of success. You're living in integrity with who you truly are. You also uncovered the truth behind self-sabotage, that it's not weakness, but a form of protection, a younger part of you, trying to stay safe. And now, instead of fighting that part, you've learned how to meet it with compassion. You understand that those moments aren't proof you're failing. They're proof you're growing.

Your blueprint began here. Not as a rigid plan, but as a rhythm. A rhythm that fits your life, a framework that supports your nervous system, a path that evolves with your growth. You created something that isn't about doing more, but about living more honestly. A structure that supports your nervous system and reflects the truth of your path. You named your anchors. You clarified your *why*. You created a living agreement with the person you are becoming.

This isn't about being perfect. It's about being present.

And when you lose your footing, which you will from time to time, you now know how to come back. Not to who you were, but to the version of you who's learning, choosing, and becoming with more grace every day. That is your practice. That is your blueprint.

And if this chapter whispered one thing, it was this: You don't have to be perfect to begin again. You just have to notice. To pause. To remember what matters. And then choose the next right step.

Your blueprint doesn't promise you won't forget. It gives you a way to come back.

And that, more than anything, is the practice of coming back to you.

CHAPTER 11

Becoming the Best Version of You

Personal Story: A Moment of Reflection Where I Saw How Far I Had Come

There are moments along the healing journey when you realize just how far you have come. They do not always arrive with fanfare. Sometimes, they arrive in the quiet knowing that you are no longer willing to abandon yourself. Some moments of healing announce themselves loudly. Others arrive so quietly, you almost miss them, until you realize something inside you has shifted for good.

For me, one of those moments came years after I stayed in an environment that once caused me deep harm. When the ownership changed at my workplace, it felt like a doorway opening just as I was preparing to walk away. I had endured years of sexual harassment, manipulation, and emotional abuse under the original founder. I had come to a breaking point, ready to leave, but then, there was something new. The founder, the one who had caused so much harm throughout the years, was finally stepping out. His son was taking over. There was hope in that moment, the fragile kind, the kind you want to trust even when your body knows better. It felt like a turning point, a chance for things to be different.

But as the new leadership settled in, old patterns began to resurface: fear over trust, control over collaboration, pressure over peace. The founder was no longer in the building. But the imprint he had left, the fear-based tendencies, remained.

I stayed. Not because I had to, but because I wanted to believe things could be different. I wanted to believe healing could happen from the inside out. For four more years, I poured my heart into trying to shift the culture. I tried to lead by example and to foster a healthier environment where people could feel safe, seen, and supported. I leaned into the work, into the culture, into the people around me. And for a while, it seemed like it might be enough.

But healing does not come just because the names change. Fear does not dissolve because leadership shifts. Slowly, the same old patterns began to creep back in, quieter perhaps, but still there. Control. Fear. Pressure that sat heavy in the air. It was different, but not different enough.

Even knowing the founder was gone, my body still reacted when I walked into that building. My shoulders would tense before I even realized it. My stomach would churn without warning. Anxiety would rise up through my chest and catch in my throat. No matter how much my mind wanted to move forward, my body remembered everything. My nervous system did not care about the paperwork. I told myself I was strong enough now, that I could simply turn away if I ever crossed paths with him, that the past was behind me. But healing is not about pretending the past never happened. It is about honoring what your body still carries and listening when it speaks.

I did the work. I talked to my therapist. I leaned on my coach, my husband, and friends who understood the layers of recovery that come after the event itself. I told my stories, sometimes in that oversharing-trauma-response way, trying to feel

> *I told my stories, sometimes in that oversharing-trauma-response way, trying to feel heard, trying to explain the invisible weight I still carried.*

heard, trying to explain the invisible weight I still carried. I stayed with the new ownership longer than I stayed for myself. I wanted so badly to believe that I could fix it. That if I showed up differently, everything would change.

There was a work event I chose to attend early on, even though the founder would be present. I prepared myself in all the ways I knew how, like quiet reassurances whispered into the stillness of early mornings. *You are safe now. You can do this.* I went, steady on the outside, even though my insides were braced for impact. I stayed aware, kept my distance, told myself I could handle it, and I did. It was not easy. He kept his distance. I kept mine. Every muscle stayed on alert until, finally, slowly, I could breathe again. But I realized then that healing is not about pretending you are unaffected. It is about giving yourself the tools to move through the discomfort without losing yourself again.

That night was not about proving anything to anyone else. It was about proving something to myself: that I could walk through an old battlefield and not lose myself again.

Later, there was another choice. An opportunity that would have placed me in closer proximity. This time, I said no. Not out of fear, but out of love. A quiet kind of love, the kind that no longer needed an audience or an explanation. I chose not to put myself back into an environment that asked me to betray my body's signals in order to keep the peace. It was the kind of love that simply says, *I do not owe anyone my discomfort to prove my strength.*

For four more years, I stayed, trying to make the best of what was left. Trying to shift the culture from within. But the deeper work of healing taught me something I had been slow to accept. Some systems do not want to change. Some environments are built on fear so deeply rooted that it is not my responsibility to fix them. I realized that healing sometimes means staying when it is right, and leaving when it no longer is.

Leaving was not a moment of defeat. It was a moment of deep clarity. I was not walking away because I had failed. I was walking away because I had learned to listen to myself, to trust my nervous system, to believe that my peace mattered more than anyone else's expectations. That choice, perhaps more than any other, showed me who I had become.

I chose myself.
That was the real
victory.

It took time to see it. But looking back now, I can see how every small choice added up. Every time I said no when it would have been easier to say yes. Every time I chose presence over programming. Every time I trusted the quiet wisdom rising in my body instead of the old voice telling me to endure. I no longer needed an apology to heal. I no longer needed approval to walk away.

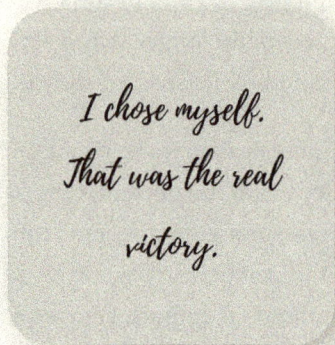

I chose myself. That was the real victory. That was the moment I realized I had become the woman I used to hope I would one day be.

And when I finally left that company altogether, it was not with resentment. It was with clarity. I realized I was never responsible for fixing a system that did not want to heal itself. I was responsible for honoring the life I was still building. A life where my peace mattered. Where my nervous system mattered. Where I mattered.

That was the moment I saw it clearly: I was not who I used to be. I had become someone I was proud to be. Not perfect. Not unscarred.

But free.

Reflecting on Who You've Become and What's Next

Healing is not about becoming someone new. It is about remembering who you have always been underneath the layers of fear, proving, and survival.

When I look back at the woman I was when I first stepped onto this path, I see someone who wanted so badly to do it right. To be enough. To prove her worth. Every achievement, every yes, every effort was another attempt to outrun the voice that said, *You have to earn your place.* But something shifted along the way. Not all at once. Not through one breakthrough. Through years of choosing, pausing, listening, and learning. Through heartbreak and healing. Through small, steady returns to myself.

> The body keeps the score, yes, but the body also keeps the story of healing.

The qualities that have grown within me are the ones that were always waiting for permission to lead: trusting my gut, trusting my spirit, trusting that my body holds wisdom my mind cannot always explain. I no longer seek validation outside of myself. I no longer feel the need to perform my worth through overachievement or perfectionism.

I have become kinder. Less judgmental. More curious about life and people, including myself. Integrity has become a guidepost rather than a goal. Worthiness is no longer something I chase. It is something I honor.

And as I look forward, I feel an openness that I never used to allow. I am no longer rushing to "get there." I am open to the changes that unfold naturally within me. Every day, every encounter, every choice, becomes another opportunity to lean more fully into who I am becoming.

When we reflect on our growth through the lens of the mind and body, we can see the nervous system healing alongside the mind. Where there used to be contraction, tension in the shoulders, a racing heart, a tight gut, there is now more ease. More breath. More openness. The body keeps the score, yes, but the body also keeps the story of healing. When we learn to trust ourselves again, we are also retraining our nervous system to experience safety, trust, and expansion in the present moment.

Research on neuroplasticity supports this truth. Studies show that reflective practices, such as self-inquiry and gratitude, help strengthen new neural pathways associated with self-trust, emotional regulation, and resilience. According to Dr. Rick Hanson's work on positive neuroplasticity, when we intentionally notice and internalize small experiences of worthiness and self-compassion, we are literally "rewiring" the brain to default toward self-respect and peace rather than fear and reactivity (2013).

Transformation does not only happen when we act differently. It happens when we *feel* differently in our bodies and believe differently in our minds. This is the real work. This is how we come back to ourselves.

Before you turn the page, take a moment to honor how far you have come. Reflection is part of the process of returning to yourself. Let these questions guide you inward, not as a test, but as a gentle reminder of your own growth.

Reflection Questions:

When I look back at where I began this journey, what part of myself has grown the most, even if it feels small?

_____

_____

_____

_____

What inner strengths have I uncovered that I did not fully trust or recognize before?

_____

_____

_____

_____

As I move forward, how can I honor who I am becoming with more kindness, presence, and trust?

_____

_____

_____

_____

Trusting the Process, the Growth, and Yourself

There is a point in every healing journey when you realize that growth does not happen because you control it. It happens because you trust it. For a long time, I believed that if I could just plan enough, prepare enough, and work hard enough, I could guarantee the outcome. I thought safety lived in control. But the truth I have come to know is that true safety, the kind that lasts, lives in trust.

When I look back at my journey, I can see the growth that happened even in moments when I doubted everything. It showed up in how I began to respond differently to difficult situations, not with panic or anger, but with presence. It showed up in how I treated people, with more compassion and patience, even when it was hard. It showed up in how I learned to let go of the things, and even the people, that no longer served my true self.

These shifts were not born from force. They were born from trust. Small choices, repeated over time, that brought me back to the version of myself that was always there, waiting beneath the noise. When challenges arise now, I meet them differently. I do not rush to fix or control. I pause. I breathe. I come back to the present moment. I remind myself of how far I have already come. I remember that everything I need is already within me. I do not have to prove anything to anyone, not even to myself.

Trusting myself does not just happen in my mind. I feel it in my body. It feels like freedom at its core. A deep knowing that no matter what happens, I will not abandon myself again. It feels like safety. Not the safety of controlling every detail, but the safety of knowing I will honor myself through whatever comes. Giving myself permission to evolve without needing all the answers has been one of the greatest gifts of this journey. I no longer demand certainty before I take the next step. I know that every time I have chosen to trust my inner knowing, it has led me back to myself. It has led me deeper into a life that feels honest, grounded, and real.

To trust the next steps, even before I see where they lead, is to truly live. It is choosing to move forward from a place of presence instead of fear. It is trusting that life is not something to survive or manage, but something to experience.

Trust is not just an idea. It is a full-body experience. When we begin to trust ourselves, our nervous system shifts from chronic vigilance into states of openness and rest. The shoulders soften. The breath deepens. The heartbeat steadies. The body learns that it does not need to brace for impact all the time. It can rest. It can open. It can respond from presence instead of protection.

The science of self-trust is supported by research in somatic psychology and neuroscience. Studies show that practices like mindfulness, breathwork, and body awareness regulate the amygdala, the part of the brain responsible for fear responses, and strengthen the prefrontal cortex, the center of conscious choice and resilience. According to research on emotional regulation, individuals who develop body-based awareness are better able to navigate uncertainty and recover from challenges with greater ease.

Trust, both in ourselves and in life, is not just emotional. It is physiological. It is something we can build, one breath, one choice at a time. Every breath you take with presence is a reminder: You are already whole.

You are already coming back to yourself.

Reflection Questions:

What is one moment in my journey where I trusted myself even when the outcome was uncertain, and how did that choice bring me closer to who I truly am?

_____

_____

_____

_____

How does my body tell me when I am living in trust versus living in fear, and how can I listen more closely?

_____

_____

_____

_____

The Power of Sharing Your Journey — How Transformation Ripples Outward

There's a moment in the healing process when you realize that your story is not just your own. By speaking the truths you once kept hidden, you offer others a pathway — not to replicate your experience, but to walk their own path with more courage, more clarity,

> I began to understand that healing is not just something we do in isolation. It's something we invite others into by being real about what it looks like.

and more compassion. Sharing my story hasn't always been easy. In fact, it used to feel terrifying. Vulnerability opens the door to judgment, to misunderstanding, and to being too much or not enough in someone else's eyes. But the more I shared, the more I noticed something else rising alongside the fear: freedom.

I no longer needed to carry the weight of guilt, shame, or secrecy. I didn't need to overexplain or justify what I had lived through. I didn't need to edit myself to be more acceptable. With every truth I spoke, first in small circles, then with clients, then on stages and pages, I felt the weight lift. I began to understand that healing is not just something we do in isolation. It's something we invite others into by being real about what it looks like. When I tell my story, I'm not just offering a timeline of events. I'm offering the possibility that you, too, can find your way back to yourself. That you are not alone in your fear, your grief, your shame, and your silence. That even if our stories don't match detail for detail, they might still mirror a feeling you've known. And in that recognition, something softens. Something opens.

What I once felt afraid to share has become the very thing that sets others free. Owning my truth without apology has created more space for others to own theirs. I no longer try to hide the parts of me that once felt heavy. I've learned to carry them with care, and in doing so, I've lightened the load for others, too. There is power in storytelling, not because it fixes anything, but because it connects us. It reminds us that we are not broken. That healing is not a competition. That every one of us has something to teach, something to release, and something to reclaim.

When we show up fully, we give others permission to do the same. Even in small ways—a moment of honesty, a quiet post, a heartfelt conversation—we become a mirror that reflects possibility, not perfection. When we share from an embodied place, it's not just the story that transmits. It's the energy. Our nervous system, once wired for hiding and protection, begins to associate vulnerability with safety instead of danger. The body starts to trust that it's okay to be seen, that expression is no longer a threat, but a pathway to connection and repair.

Neuroscience shows us that storytelling activates multiple regions of the brain. Not only the language centers, but also areas connected to empathy, emotional processing, and memory. When we hear someone's story, we don't just understand it. We feel it. This is why shared vulnerability has been shown to increase oxytocin, the "connection hormone," which helps regulate stress and build trust. When we share from a grounded, authentic place, we create safety for ourselves and for others.

Every time I speak my truth, I feel myself return. Every time someone tells me, "I saw myself in your story," I remember why it matters. The ripples may start quietly. But they spread.

Reflection Questions:

What part of my journey am I ready to share, not to explain or justify, but to connect and invite healing in myself or someone else?

_____

_____

_____

_____

CRYSTAL ROBINSON

How might sharing my truth, even in small ways, create space for someone else to feel safe, seen, or inspired?

_____

_____

_____

_____

Sometimes we don't realize the impact of our healing until we see it reflected in someone else's eyes. The quiet "me too" in a conversation. The way someone softens when they hear your story. The way you no longer shrink when sharing it. That's when it becomes clear that the work you've done hasn't stayed contained. It's moved. It's echoed. It's rippled outward in ways you'll never fully know.

You might not see the lives you've touched. You may never hear the words of someone who made a different choice because of something you once said out loud. But it's happening. Healing rarely ends with you. It moves through you. And now, as you stand here; not at a finish line, but in the middle of your journey, there's a quiet invitation. Not to do more. Not to be better. Just to name it. To acknowledge how far you've come and the direction in which you're choosing to move from here.

Because even when the path ahead is unclear, the compass is inside you. And sometimes, the most powerful way to move forward is simply to declare: I trust myself now. I know who I am. And I am willing to keep choosing myself, one moment at a time.

Final Action Step: A Commitment to Your Future Self

There's a moment, after all the reflecting, after the releasing, after the returning, when you feel the quiet rise of something new. It's not a breakthrough. It's not a dramatic declaration. It's the slow inhale of self-trust. The kind that says, *I'm still here. And I'm still choosing me.*

This is where we honor that choice.

Not because everything is perfect now. But because you've come back to yourself enough times to know you always can. You've felt the shifts in your body, in your thoughts, and in your way of showing up, and even if you're still in the middle of the process, you know now that the process is yours to hold.

So before you turn the page and step into what's next, take a moment to speak directly to the version of you who will return to this book one day, perhaps a year from now. The one who might need a reminder. The one who may have forgotten how far you've already come.

Write A Letter to Your Future Self

Not a list of goals, not a plan—a letter. From the version of you, who knows what it feels like to come home to yourself. Seal it. Hide it in a drawer. Tuck it into a book. Set a reminder on your calendar to open it a year from now.

This is not about performance. It's about presence. It's about saying, *I see you. I trust you. I'll keep coming back for you.* Let it be honest. Let it be loving. Let it be yours.

You don't need to get the words perfect. Just be honest. You might write about what you've learned, what you're still holding, or what you're ready to let go of. You might want to name the patterns that no longer have power over you, or the small rituals that keep bringing you back to center. Maybe you'll write about who you're becoming, or maybe you'll just describe how it feels to be you, right now, in this moment of truth, tenderness, and trust.

Let this be a conversation with the version of yourself who might need these words when the road feels unclear again.

Summary: Returning to Yourself: The Quiet Power of Remembering Who You Are

I just said no. That quiet kind of "no" that carries years of healing behind it.

Some chapters don't end with answers. They end with a breath. With a return. This one began quietly. Not with transformation as a destination, but with a moment of pause. The kind that arrives not when everything is solved, but when you've finally stopped abandoning yourself in order to belong somewhere that never felt safe to begin with.

I didn't leave the place where I had been harmed. Not right away. I stayed. I hoped. I gave it everything I had, thinking maybe I could shift it from the inside out. When the man who hurt me left and his son took over, I told myself it could be the beginning of something new. But my nervous system knew the truth before my mind could admit it. Even without his presence, the imprint lingered. The fear in the room. The tension in my body. The dread I couldn't explain. My body remembered, and eventually, I listened.

That was a moment. Not a loud one. Not a triumphant one. But one that changed everything. The moment I chose to honor what I knew inside, instead of what I hoped might change outside. The moment I said no, not because I was afraid, but because I loved myself too much to stay in a place that asked me to betray my own body's wisdom. And later, when another choice appeared, one that would have placed me too close to old harm, I didn't need to prove my strength. I just said no. That quiet kind of "no" that carries years of healing behind it.

These are the moments that shape us. Not the grand gestures, but the quiet returns, the small decisions to trust ourselves again and again. There was science behind what I was learning, though I didn't always know it at the time. My nervous system was unlearning old patterns of bracing and collapsing. My brain was forming new pathways. Research in somatic healing and neuroplasticity confirms it. Healing is not just emotional. It's cellular. Every time I paused, every time I breathed instead of reacted, every time I chose to rest rather than push through, I was teaching my body that safety was possible. That trust was safe to feel.

I began to see that trust was not just something I gave to other people. It was something I had to give to myself. That's what this chapter has held: the recognition that I didn't need to perform for my peace. That I could choose a different rhythm—one rooted in presence—one that allowed me to step into situations with awareness or walk away with love and never feel like I was losing myself in either decision.

You've walked alongside me in these pages. Not just in the story of leaving a toxic workplace, but in the story underneath it. The story of remembering my worth. Of reclaiming my voice. Of no longer needing an apology to heal or permission to be free. And maybe, somewhere in my story, you've seen glimpses of your own.

Maybe you've noticed how you breathe differently when you think about a decision you made that honored your truth. Maybe you've remembered the moment you didn't shrink, the moment you spoke up or the moment you walked away or stayed for the right reasons. That's the work. That's the return.

It's never just about the past. It's about how you carry yourself now. And how, in doing so, you become a quiet reflection for others. Not because you're trying to teach. But because you're living in your truth.

This chapter doesn't end with a neat conclusion. It ends with a letter. One written by you, for you, because no one else can mark your progress like you can. This is not a letter for a stranger to read. It's for the part of you who might forget. The part that will need reminding. The part that still aches sometimes and just wants to know that it's doing okay. So write it. Seal it. Hide it if you must. Just don't forget what it means.

You are not becoming. You are returning.

To yourself. For yourself. Always.

CHAPTER 12

The Journey Continues: Living & Embodying Mission Me 2.0

Personal Story: A Moment When I Fully Embraced My Transformation and Saw the Impact of My Work

There's a moment in healing that no one really prepares you for. Not the breakthrough. Not the insight. Not even the moment you finally feel like yourself again. It's what comes after all of that. When life invites you to *live* the work you've done. Not in a controlled environment or when everything is calm, but in real time, in unpredictable situations, with people who don't know the version of you you've fought so hard to become. Not in a circle of safe support or in the quiet comfort of solitude. But in the messy, raw, unscripted moments where no one else sees you and your old wounds whisper, *"prove yourself."* These moments are not announcements. They don't arrive with clarity or confidence. Often, they come as tension. As discomfort. As a trigger you thought you'd healed long ago.

One of the first times I realized I was truly living the Mission Me 2.0 framework happened with my son, but not in the way I expected. He was heading off to college, stepping into a season that was supposed to be filled with pride and celebration, but what unfolded instead was pain I wasn't ready for.

He had finished high school in the middle of the pandemic, a time of isolation and uncertainty, when even the most grounded teenagers struggled to stay connected to themselves. He had been questioning his identity, his emotions, and his place in the world. And slowly, the closeness we once shared began to shift. He was navigating his own questions about who he was and how to exist in a world that had completely unraveled during the pandemic.

One day, he stopped hugging me completely—no touching, no goodbye hug, no soft moment before he left for six months. He couldn't give it, and I didn't know how to make peace with that. At first, I brushed it off. *He's a teenager*, I thought. *He needs space.* But the space became silence. And the silence became distance.

He left for college without a goodbye hug. Six months. No embrace. No squeeze of reassurance. No familiar gesture to anchor the moment. It might seem small to someone else, but to me, it was a heartbreak I didn't know how to process. For over a year, he refused hugs or any kind of touch.

At first, I tried to be patient. Then, I tried to rationalize. Eventually, I begged. I felt like I had done something terribly wrong as a mother. I questioned everything. I told myself it was a phase. I tried to be understanding. But inside, I was unraveling. I begged for connection. I questioned everything I'd done as a mother. Was it me? Had I pushed too hard? Not shown up enough? Was I being punished for something I didn't even understand? Was I too much? Not enough? Had I failed him? Was I unworthy of connection?

He would leave the house, and I would replay every interaction. I'd sit in the ache of that emptiness, stewing for days, trying to find the missing piece that would make sense of it all. I would sit in silence, overanalyzing everything I ever did as a mom. Even after he returned, the weight of those thoughts didn't lift. Weeks turned into months, and I was still trying to figure out what I could've done differently. That pattern lasted for over a year.

Eventually, it broke me. The heartbreak became too big to hold quietly. I was unable to hold it in any longer. There was no grace in my grief, no polished reflection—just me, sobbing in my bedroom, crying so hard I couldn't stop. I slid to the floor, where grief overtook my entire body. I remember crawling to the bathroom, my stomach in knots, crying so hard I vomited. I was shaking. From the heaving, I wet my pants. I couldn't catch my breath. I sobbed like the mother I was: broken and undone, mourning a goodbye that had never come. It was one of the lowest, most vulnerable moments of my life.

I realized I was making his boundary about my worth. And that had to stop.

But somewhere in the middle of all that, in the heartbreak, the guilt, the shame, the crying, the purging, and the surrender, something shifted. I found something deeper than pain. I found the edge of something I needed to understand: that his boundaries weren't a reflection of my failure but of his becoming. And I needed to let him go without making it about me. I realized I was making his boundary about my worth.

And that had to stop. That was embodiment—not in the pretty way, but in the messy, raw, unspiritual way that real growth often arrives. I began to understand that it wasn't about me. His detachment was part of *his* process, not a punishment for mine. Honoring his boundaries, even when they hurt, was part of my healing. Love doesn't always look like closeness. Sometimes, it looks like space.

Eventually, he came back to me. The hugs returned, slowly, gently, in his own time. And when they did, I received them with a kind of gratitude I hadn't known before. But the real healing had happened long before the hugs returned. The healing happened the moment I stopped chasing the version of motherhood I thought I had to perform and allowed myself to feel the grief of being human inside it. That's embodiment.

Not the version we post online. The version that happens on the bathroom floor when no one's watching. The kind that breaks something open inside you, so something truer can rise. And just when I thought I had lived through the hardest part, life handed me another mirror. This time, at work.

This moment was quieter but equally revealing.

There was a coworker I interacted with regularly, and from the very beginning, something about our exchanges always felt off. Every interaction seemed to escalate. He would get accusatory quickly, and defensive, intense, and overly detailed in ways that felt disproportionate to the conversation. He'd talk over people, jump to conclusions, and argue small points with a kind of urgency that didn't match the tone of the room. It got under my skin in a way I couldn't explain. I'd leave those meetings unsettled. My chest would tighten. My patience would fray. And I'd find myself rehearsing what I *should've* said long after the meeting had ended.

For a while, I told myself he was just difficult. But something deeper was being stirred, something familiar. He overexplained, became emotionally charged, and I recognized it immediately. So, I paused. I sat with the discomfort. And I asked a question I had learned to ask when something kept poking at my peace: *What is this actually about?* And then I saw it.

It was me. Or rather, it *had been* me.

Not long ago, I had been that person. The one who felt misunderstood, constantly needing to prove herself, always on edge, waiting to be criticized. I remembered the feeling of walking into meetings bracing for attack, of overexplaining because I didn't feel safe, and of reacting from fear instead of grounded presence. That was the fear I used to carry. That was the old version of myself I had spent years healing from.

It was me.

Or rather,

it had been me.

I saw my shadow in him. And in that moment, I didn't feel superior. I felt compassion. Not because his behavior was acceptable—it wasn't—but because I understood it. I had lived it. I knew the cost of being in that state, the way it steals your joy and warps your perception. And more importantly, I knew what it took to move through it. I didn't try to fix him. I didn't take it personally. And I didn't collapse under the pressure of trying to manage the situation. But I didn't react either. I held space. I breathed. I understood. I stayed regulated. I stayed kind. And I stayed whole.

That's how I knew the work was working.

Reflection on Growth: How Far You Have Come

When we first started this journey together, maybe you didn't know exactly what you were seeking. If you think back to when you first picked up this book, maybe you can remember the feeling you were carrying. Maybe you just knew you were tired of the noise. Of the grind. Of the way life kept asking you to show up for everything and everyone but yourself. Maybe you weren't even sure you were ready for something different, only that you couldn't keep carrying the weight the same way anymore.

Maybe you didn't notice it at first. Maybe the shifts were small, almost invisible from the outside. A breath you stayed with instead of rushing past. A boundary you honored, even though every part of you wanted to apologize. A moment of discomfort you sat through without numbing or fixing or running.

And then came the quiet realization – that you couldn't keep carrying the weight the same way anymore. I remember carrying that same weight, the constant pressure to do more, to be more, to prove. I was holding it all together even when I was unraveling inside. I didn't know exactly what I needed back then. I just knew I couldn't survive much longer inside the life I had built around everyone else's needs but my own.

Maybe you found yourself crying over something you would have stuffed down a year ago. Maybe you caught yourself laughing, really laughing, without waiting for permission. Maybe you stood a little taller. Breathed a little deeper. Asked a question you once would have been too afraid to voice. Maybe nothing around you changed, not at first, but something inside you softened. Opened. Trusted a little more.

> *Easier to tell yourself this is just the way life is, than to pause and ask, but what if it's not?*

And now, here you are.

You've made it through the work that most people never even begin. Not because they are incapable, but because it's easier to stay busy than to sit still. Easier to numb than to feel. Easier to tell yourself *this is just the way life is*, than to pause and ask, *but what if it's not?*

But you did. You paused. You looked inward. You faced things that were not easy to name. You listened to your body's wisdom instead of overriding it. You softened toward yourself instead of hardening further. You returned to your breath, to your truth, to your own center. Maybe it didn't happen all at once. Maybe it was one small decision, then another. Maybe it was recognizing your own patterns and offering yourself compassion instead of criticism. Maybe it was catching yourself in an old reaction and choosing presence instead of panic.

I remember a moment like that, realizing I could sit in the heartbreak of my son pulling away, not by making it about what I had done wrong, but by letting him have his space without it collapsing my own sense of worth. I didn't fix it by controlling it. I healed by allowing it.

This is how it happens, real transformation. Not in grand declarations. Not in neatly tied-up breakthroughs. But in the ordinary, sacred work of returning to yourself, moment by moment. Every small shift matters. Every time you choose curiosity over judgment. Every time you stay with yourself through discomfort instead of abandoning yourself. Every time you honor your boundaries, even when it feels unfamiliar or scary.

This is growth.

Maybe now, looking back, you can see the difference. Not because you have a new title. Not because your life looks perfectly arranged on the outside. Not the kind that shows up in highlight reels. The kind that roots itself deep beneath the surface and makes everything stronger. You didn't need to become someone new. You just needed to remember who you already were underneath the survival patterns and the noise.

And now you carry that remembering with you. Not as a perfect destination, but as a living, breathing relationship with yourself, one that will continue to deepen every time you choose to stay connected, even when life gets loud again. You are proof that healing is not just possible. It's already happening.

Because you can feel it. The steadiness where there used to be scrambling, the breath where there used to be bracing, the tenderness where there used to be judgment. You didn't have to force it. You didn't have to earn it. You simply chose to stay. You chose to listen. You chose to come back—again and again. And that choice changed everything.

Integration: How To Keep Applying the Lessons from the Book in Everyday Life

Healing isn't something you finish. It's something you carry. It's something you live, a little more honestly, a little more bravely, every day. As you move forward, it's not about holding onto every detail or trying to perfect every practice. It's about remembering what you felt along the way and trusting yourself enough to keep choosing it, even when no one is watching.

Let's pause here, at this threshold between what you've explored and what you're about to live, and look back for a moment. Not to measure or grade. But to honor. There's a way you begin to notice the work settling into your bones, even when life doesn't hand you a medal for it. It's not in the grand moments. It's in the ordinary ones. The breath before you react. The question you ask instead of the judgment you used to land on. The softening in your chest where there used to be armor.

It was never just about thinking differently. It was about learning to live differently. To listen differently.

When you think back to where we began, back to the early pages of this book, maybe you remember the disconnection. The busyness. The feeling of moving through life in a fog you could barely name. Mindset alone could not fix that. It was never just about thinking differently. It was about learning to live differently. To listen differently. Each chapter is a piece of your return. Each story is an invitation. Each insight is a thread you can weave into your own way of being.

In the beginning, we named the feeling that brought you here, the quiet ache that said there must be more than survival. We talked about how healing happens when science and spirituality stop competing and start collaborating. I shared how my own healing truly began when I stopped trying to "think" my way out of pain, and instead, trusted the language of my body and spirit. We started by weaving together two worlds, science and soul, because healing lives in both. You saw how the nervous system speaks its own language and how survival mode wires the brain to protect, not to thrive. You also saw how your spirit had never given up on you, whispering, nudging, and calling you back. Transformation doesn't happen through force. It happens through integration.

In Chapter 2, we faced the noise together, the autopilot living, the disconnection, and the survival patterns we've normalized. I told you how I lived in that grind for years, believing exhaustion was simply part of being successful. I shared how I stopped trying to "think positive" through my own breakdowns and started honoring the sacred information my body was carrying. Science reminded me I wasn't crazy. Spirit reminded me I wasn't broken. Awareness is the first step. You can't heal what you won't name.

We peeled back the layers of emotional suppression and survival responses. I shared how long I kept performing strength, believing vulnerability was weakness, until my body finally made me listen.

You moved from awareness into embodiment, one layer at a time. You felt how survival patterns—the constant fight, flight, freeze—don't dissolve just because we wish them away. They shift when we build safety, when we regulate, and when we create small enough steps that the brain says "yes" instead of shutting down. Maybe you remembered moments when your own body whispered *enough*. When your spirit felt too heavy to carry alone. When you realized you didn't have to earn your worth by holding everything together. Feeling is not a flaw. It's a return to life.

We talked about the body, how it holds the truth when the mind tries to rewrite the story. I remembered the years of ignoring the warning signs until illness forced me to stop. You saw how your body is not the enemy. It is the map. The nervous system is not betraying you. It's trying to keep you alive. And slowly, through breath, through movement, and through space, you taught it that safety was possible again. Your body is not betraying you. It's trying to bring you home. We explored the nervous system, the constant state of bracing for impact. I shared the moment I realized that rest wasn't a reward to be earned, but a necessity for survival. Regulation is not indulgence. It's the foundation for everything.

Boundaries. Worth. Self-respect. I told you about the years I said yes when I meant no, and how reclaiming my "no" was an act of love, not rebellion. Boundaries are not walls. They are bridges back to yourself.

We talked about mindset and how it's not enough on its own. I shared how positive thinking became a mask until I allowed myself to confront the beliefs underneath. True change happens when thought, feeling, and action come into alignment.

Boundaries are not walls. They are bridges back to yourself.

We sat with the idea of growth not being linear. I told you about the setbacks that weren't really setbacks at all, just invitations to deepen the work. You explored your relationship to your emotions, not to fix them, but to feel them. You learned that anger can be sacred. That grief has wisdom. That joy doesn't need justification. I told you about the times I sat on my bathroom floor, feeling like I would break under the weight of feeling, and how that breaking was not the end, it was the beginning. Progress is not a straight line. It's a living, breathing process.

We explored resilience, not the polished kind, but the kind built in the messy, broken places. I shared the story of standing in the mirror and finally seeing strength in my own reflection. You stood face to face with your shadow. You saw the parts of yourself that once felt unlovable, the parts that overworked, overgave, and overexplained, and instead of judging them, you softened. You held them. You grew because of them, not in spite of them. You made peace with imperfection. You chose your own timing. You stopped waiting for someone else's permission to rest, to breathe, to belong to yourself. Strength is not in how little you bend. It's in how deeply you root.

We built something together: a living, flexible blueprint. I shared how I created rhythms that honored my real life, not the one I thought I "should" have. You rebuilt your blueprint, not a rigid one, but a living, breathing one that evolves with you. One where daily practices became anchors, not shackles. One where rhythm matters more than routine. One where honoring your needs is not selfishness—it's alignment. Your healing doesn't need to look impressive. It needs to feel true.

We circled back to presence and the idea that transformation isn't about becoming someone else. It's about returning to the version of you that always existed underneath the survival patterns. I shared how, even now, I am still learning, still softening, and still choosing myself over the old programs. And maybe, without even realizing it, you've started to live differently. You listened when your body said no. You stayed when your mind wanted to flee. You softened where you once would have braced. Healing is not a one-time event. It's a relationship with yourself. This is the work.

It is not about becoming someone else. It is about becoming available to the version of you who was always whole, the one who remembers, in your cells and spirit, that healing is not a destination. It is a way of walking. It is a way of breathing. It is a way of being. Because every breath you take with more presence, every boundary you honor with more courage, every time you offer yourself tenderness instead of punishment, you are living the work—not chasing it, not performing it. Living it.

This is Mission Me 2.0.

Reflection Questions:

What are the small signs in my daily life that show me I am returning to myself?

_____

_____

_____

_____

Where do I still feel tempted to hustle, to perform, to earn my worth, and what would it feel like to soften there?

_____

_____

_____

_____

Embracing Change

Understanding That Transformation is an Evolving Process, Not a Single Moment, but a Living Process

There are moments now when I catch myself doing something so simple, and yet, I feel it. The shift. Noticing that my breath is steady, even in a room that used to make me hold it. Pausing before I speak, and actually hearing what I want to say, not what I think will keep the peace. Choosing to walk away from an old pattern instead of explaining it one more time. Letting someone be exactly who they are without making it mean something about me. If I had written this chapter years ago, I think I would've tried to end with clarity, with some kind of answer or lesson that tied it all together.

But the truth is, the deeper I've gone into my own healing, the less I believe in tidy endings. Transformation has never been a single moment for me. It's something I live, again and again. I don't wake up every day with a perfectly aligned routine or a magical sense of peace, but I do wake up differently.

None of these moments announce themselves. They don't feel like breakthroughs. They feel like presence. And that's what's different now. I live my life from this space of coming back, again and again, to myself. It's not that I don't get triggered. I still do. It's not that I don't forget the tools. I do that, too. But I notice sooner. I stay longer. I soften quicker. And I remember that none of this has a finish line.

There's no longer urgency in my mornings. No rush to get ahead or prove anything to anyone. Some days, I catch myself before I fall into old patterns. The version of me that used to chase approval, I still see her sometimes. The version of me that begged for connection and collapsed under silence, still lives in my body. But now, I meet her with compassion. I don't force her to disappear. I hold her hand, and we keep walking. Other days, I don't. But even then, I notice sooner. I come back faster. I soften more easily.

It's the way you sit with your own discomfort, the way you breathe through a conversation that once would've flattened you.

This work, this way of living, is not a program to complete. It's a rhythm you learn to follow. It's the way you sit with your own discomfort, the way you breathe through a conversation that once would've flattened you. It's knowing your nervous system doesn't need to prepare for a war when someone has a different opinion. This is healing. This is change.

I pause more before I speak most of the time. I think more about what I truly want to say. And I listen differently—not to fix, not to agree or disagree, just to understand. There was a time I thought I had to explain myself to everyone. Now, I see most people are speaking from their own experiences, and I don't need to defend mine. I'm learning to live from the truth of my own lived experience, even as it continues to evolve. It's how I live now when I honor my body. When I hold a boundary, even when it still feels like a wall. When I stop before reacting. When I remember that everyone is carrying their own story. And that I don't need to carry the weight of theirs to live the truth of mine. Even with my son, now older, more open, more himself, I still feel those little echoes of the mother I used to be. And when they rise, I don't silence them. I sit with her, too. I thank her for doing her best.

That, to me, is healing. Not a destination. Not an endpoint. But a feeling of returning, again and again, with compassion, awareness, and enough breath to choose differently. You may have found that, too. Your own rhythm. Maybe you don't need the urgency anymore. Maybe you find yourself asking better questions. Maybe you've stopped needing to be understood in order to feel grounded.

And maybe the biggest shift isn't anything others can see. Maybe it's the way you're listening to yourself now. The way you hold your boundaries, even when they feel misunderstood. The way you've stopped needing to prove anything to anyone, even yourself. We are always unfolding.

There will be new triggers. New stories. New places where the ground feels unfamiliar again. But now you know how to stay with yourself through those places. Even at work, I still meet parts of myself I've already outgrown. Not because I failed to heal them, but because life keeps offering me new ways to meet them with grace. And even now, in this moment, writing this final chapter... I know I'm not done. I'm still returning, too.

That's what I want you to know as we come to the end of these pages: This isn't a closing. This is a continuation. You're not finishing something here. You're stepping into it. You are not behind. You are not late. You are in the process. You are walking this, breath by breath, just like I am. And even when it doesn't feel perfect, even when you forget, and even when you falter, you're not lost. You're learning. You're evolving. You're coming back.

And if you forget, you already know how to return. That's the heart of Mission Me 2.0. It's not something you become. It's something you remember. How to live freely, open, with compassion and grace. So if you're wondering what comes next, maybe just begin there. Slow down. Pause. Question everything.

Ask: *What would honoring myself look like right now?* You don't have to answer it perfectly. Just ask.

That's what I do, too. I'm so proud of you.

Reflection Invitation:

You might pause here (just for a moment), and let your own voice speak. How will I honor my healing not as a project to finish, but as a way of living, breathing, and choosing?

_____

_____

_____

_____

Who am I now, at this moment? Who am I becoming when I continue to stay present with myself?

_____

_____

_____

_____

There are no wrong answers.

Only the quiet truth that's ready to rise.

A Letter from Me to You

Dear Love,

Before you close these pages, I want to take a moment to simply sit with you — right here — in this space we've shared. I want you to know how much I see the journey you've taken. Not the polished version. Not the "after" photo. The real one. The quiet, private, steady work of choosing yourself over and over again, even when it would have been easier to forget.

I know how hard this work can feel. Not because you're doing it wrong, but because you're doing it honestly. Because you're walking through the places most people are too afraid to go. There's a kind of bravery in that. A kind of grace. If no one has told you lately, I want you to hear it from me:

I am so proud of you.

Not because you finished a book. Not because you figured everything out. But because you chose to stay with yourself when it would have been easier to turn away. You are not the same person who opened this book. Maybe the world outside hasn't noticed yet, but I believe you have. In the way you breathe. In the way you listen to your body. In the way you hold space for yourself now, even when life gets loud.

This journey we walked together wasn't about fixing what was broken. It was about remembering what was already whole inside you and giving yourself permission to live from that place again. Healing isn't a race. Transformation isn't something you achieve and hold onto forever. It's something you breathe into, grow into, and return to, again and again. This path you're walking, it doesn't end here. It keeps unfolding. And so will you.

There will be days when it feels effortless, and days when you wonder if you've forgotten everything you've learned. Please know that both are part of the journey. Both are sacred. Both are welcome. You don't have to do it perfectly. You don't have to do it alone. You are already doing it, simply by being willing to live your life a little more awake, a little more honest, and a little more you. There will be days when old stories resurface. There will be moments when you forget your own light.

When that happens, I hope you remember: You have already proven you know how to come back. To your breath. To your body. To your truth. To yourself. You have everything you need inside of you to create a life that feels happy, healthy, and fulfilled. Because that life isn't built on achievements. It's built on the quiet, daily choice to honor your true self.

I will always be cheering you on. Not just for who you are today, but for every version of you that is still unfolding. You are your greatest work. You always have been and will continue to be. And I hope you know, with your whole being, that you are not alone on this path. Not now. Not ever. I am so proud to have walked this small part of the road with you.

If you feel called, I would be honored to hear about your journey. There's something sacred about speaking your growth out loud, giving language to the quiet shifts, the small returns, and the living proof that change is real. If you would like to share what has shifted for you, how you are living your Mission Me 2.0, or what next step you are excited to embrace, you are welcome to write to me at crystallee@crystalmoonholistichealing.com.

You don't need to write anything perfect or polished. You don't need to have all the answers. Just speak from the place inside you that knows how far you've already come. I would love to celebrate with you.

You are never walking this path alone. I'll be cheering for you, quietly, fiercely, and endlessly, as you keep choosing yourself, one breath, one step, and one living moment at a time.

Love and light,
Crystal

Mission Me 2.0 Resources and Recommended Reading and Listening

This book is the result of lived experience and deep integration of science, spirituality, and story. Along the way, I've been shaped and supported by brilliant teachers, powerful research, and conversations that helped me heal. The following resources were part of that journey. My hope is that they offer you the same clarity, courage, and comfort they brought me.

Scientific and Foundational Frameworks

- **Dr. Michael Merzenich & Dr. Norman Doidge**
  Neuroplasticity and how the brain rewires through experience.
  The Brain That Changes Itself

- **Dr. Aaron Beck & Dr. Albert Ellis**
  Founders of Cognitive Behavioral Therapy (CBT).
  Reframing negative thought patterns that keep us stuck.

- **Dr. Shad Helmstetter**
  The Reticular Activating System (RAS) and how what we focus on expands.

- **Dr. Martin Seligman**
  The PERMA Model of well-being and positive psychology.
  Flourish

- **Dr. Carol Dweck**
  Growth mindset as a foundation for healing and expansion.
  Mindset

- **Dr. Joe Dispenza**
  Combining neuroscience, quantum physics, and healing.
  Becoming Supernatural

- **Dr. Sara Lazar (Harvard University)**
  Research on how mindfulness changes the brain.

- **Dr. Robert Sapolsky**
  Chronic stress, burnout, and the mind-body connection.
  Why Zebras Don't Get Ulcers

- **Dr. Stephen Porges**
  Polyvagal Theory and how nervous system regulation supports healing.

- **Dr. Jennifer Lerner & Dr. Susan David**
  Reframing fear as a growth tool.
  Harvard's "Harnessing Fear for Growth" study

- **Elliot Connie & Dr. Adam Froerer**
  Solution-Focused Brief Therapy (SFBT) and its role in possibility-based change and resilience.

- **Dr. William Miller & Dr. Stephen Rollnick**
  Motivational Interviewing (MI) and collaborative conversations that spark commitment and change.

- **Carl Jung**
  Shadow work and integrating hidden parts of the self for transformation.

- **Dr. Joseph LeDoux**
  The neuroscience of fear and how the brain responds to threat.

- **Dr. Bruce Lipton**
  Beliefs, epigenetics, and how our thoughts impact our biology.
  The Biology of Belief

- **Dr. Elizabeth Blackburn & Dr. Elissa Epel**
  Epigenetics and telomere research showing how stress and lifestyle affect longevity.

- **Deepak Chopra**
  Mind-body healing, spiritual laws of success, and Ayurvedic principles.
  How consciousness, intention, dosha balance, and meditation support long-term wellness and prevention.
  Quantum Healing, The Seven Spiritual Laws of Success, Perfect Health, The Healing Self

- **Dan Buettner**
  Purpose and longevity from global Blue Zones research.
  The Blue Zones Secrets for Living Longer

- **HeartMath Institute**
  The science of heart-brain coherence for emotional and physical healing.

- **Dr. Mihaly Csikszentmihalyi**
  Flow state and peak performance research. How presence and intentional action create transformational results.
  Flow: The Psychology of Optimal Experience

- **Dr. Richard Tedeschi & Dr. Lawrence Calhoun (1996)**
  Defined Post-Traumatic Growth (PTG) as the positive psychological change that occurs after adversity.

- **Harvard Study on Fear & Growth (2020)**
  Harnessing fear as a tool for resilience and emotional regulation.
  Reframing fear linked to lower cortisol, greater HRV, and long-term
  psychological growth.
  Researchers: Dr. Jennifer Lerner, Dr. Susan David, and colleagues
  Published in the Journal of Positive Psychology

- **Dr. Bessel van der Kolk**
  Yoga and the nervous system. Why movement, dance, yoga, and
  intuitive motion help process trauma stored in the body.
  The Body Keeps the Score

Books That Shaped My Healing
(Some are cited in Mission Me 2.0)

- *The Seven Spiritual Laws of Success* **by Deepak Chopra**
  This book gave me language for what I already believed deep within,
  that success isn't about striving, but about alignment, intention, and
  trust. Its principles are woven throughout Mission Me 2.0 and the
  way I live and guide others every day.

- *The Change: Insights into Self Empowerment, Volume 22*
  Part of *The Change* book series created by Jim Lutes and Jim Britt,
  this anthology features powerful stories of transformation and
  growth. My chapter, "The Catalyst," shares part of my personal
  journey to healing and purpose. This entire series is a testament to
  what's possible when we step into who we truly are.

- *Quantum Healing* **by Deepak Chopra**
  A foundational work exploring the connection between
  consciousness and healing. This book helped solidify the integration
  of science and soul that defines my approach to wellness and
  wholeness.

- **Anything by Deepak Chopra, Wayne Dyer, or Brené Brown**
  Their bodies of work have each contributed to my understanding of purpose, emotion, and empowerment in different seasons of life.

- *The Body Keeps the Score* by Dr. Bessel van der Kolk

- *The Meaning of Truth* by Nicole J. Sachs, LCSW

- *Untamed* by Glennon Doyle

- *Greenlights* by Matthew McConaughey

- *It Takes What It Takes* by Trevor Moawad

- *Essentialism* by Greg McKeown

- *Eat Pray Love* by Elizabeth Gilbert

- *Ikigai* by Héctor Garcia & Francesc Miralles

- *The Integrity Advantage* by Kelley Kosow

- *The Empath's Survival Guide* by Dr. Judith Orloff

- *The Blue Zones* by Dan Buettner

- *The Untethered Soul* by Michael A. Singer

Each of these books met me at a different point in my healing. Some grounded me in truth. Others challenged me to grow. All were part of coming back to myself.

Podcasts That Guided or Inspired Me
Featured Guest on:

- *Retrieving Sanity: A Mental Health Podcast*

- *Flying Upstream Podcast* with **Luisa Anderson & Kristyn Medeiros**

- *Grief, Let's Talk About It Podcast*

- *Becoming is Messy* with **Meghann Dawson**

- *Happiness Highway* with **The Less Stress Doc**

- *Vibrant Soul Society* with **Baba Sam Shelley**

- *The Mindful Movement Podcast*

- *The Mindful Soul Center Podcast*

- *Arukah Holistic Podcast* with **Mayim Vega**

- *Morning Coffee Live* with **Ondra Němčik**

- *Rich, Sexy, and Free* with **Jo Warwick**

- *Good Morning Minute* with **Angelina Mojica**

- *When Not Yet Becomes Right Now*

- *The Stubbs Show*

Podcasts I Listen To Often

- *Heal Squad* x **Maria Menounos**

- *The Mel Robbins Podcast*

- *I'd Like to Unsubscribe* with **Marisa Zeppieri and Britt Walker**

- *Deepak Chopra's Infinite Potential*

Each episode, whether I was listening or speaking, gave me language, perspective, or peace when I needed it most.

\-

Thank You for Joining Me on This Journey

I'm so grateful you chose to spend time with this book.
Whether you read it cover to cover or took what you needed, I hope
it offered something meaningful for your mind, body, or spirit.

As a heartfelt thank you, I've created a few free gifts to
support you on your path. No strings, just support.

Download your free gifts here:

Your thoughts matter deeply to me.
If this book touched you in any way, I'd love to hear from you.

Please consider leaving a review on Amazon.
It truly helps others discover what's possible for them too.
With gratitude,
Crystal

www.ingramcontent.com/pod-product-compliance
Lightning Source LLC
Chambersburg PA
CBHW032052090426
42744CB00005B/179